Contributing writer: Lisa Brooks

Photography from: Jens Bludau, Ron Cogswell; Jason Coyne; Daderot; FEMA/ Tim Burkitt; Dean Franklin; The Gates Frontiers Fund Colorado Collection, The Lyda Hill Texas Collection, The George F. Landegger Collection of District of Columbia Photographs, The Jon B. Lovelace Collection of California Photographs and The West Virginia Collection of Photographs in Carol M. Highsmith's America Project, Library of Congress, Prints and Photographs Division; Jefferson National Expansion Memorial, NPS; Balthazar Korab Archive at the Library of Congress; Conrad Lee; John Margolies Roadside America photograph archive (1972-2008), Library of Congress, Prints and Photographs Division; Library of Congress, Prints & Photographs Division, FSA/OWI Collection and Harris & Ewing Collection; National Archives and Record Administration; New York World-Telegram and the Sun Newspaper Photograph Collection; NPS; NPS/Ruben Andrade; NPS/ Brenda Schwartz; NPS/S. Smith; K. Shimada; Shutterstock.com

Louis Weber, CEO
Publications International, Ltd.
8140 Lehigh Avenue
Morton Grove, IL 60053

Permission is never granted for commercial purposes.

ISBN: 978-1-64030-153-5

Manufactured in China.

8 7 6 5 4 3 2 1

Table of Contents

Ocmulgee National Monument
Macon, Georgia

Humans first began living in the area that is now Macon, Georgia, about 17,000 years ago, during an Ice Age. They've lived there ever since. In 900 C.E., a group of American Indians called the Mississippians settled in the area. They built the mounds and a lodge that are still seen there today.

In the 1930s, during the heart of the Great Depression, Franklin Delano Roosevelt's administration set up the Works Progress Administration (WPA), as well as other programs like the Civilian Conservation Corps (CCC). Workers from these programs took part in a massive excavation project that unearthed around 2.5 million artifacts from many different time periods. The site was given National Monument status in 1936.

The entrance to the Earth Lodge is shown here. The ceilings and walls were reconstructed in the 1930, but the floor is original and dates back to 1015. The building was used for gatherings and held a fire pit and seats for fifty people.

One of the mounds at Ocmulgee. Some of the mounds were used for religious gatherings, another as a burial site.

The Lesser Temple Mound. The Great and Lesser Temple Mounds had religious and ceremonial significance.

Petroglyph National Monument
Albuquerque, New Mexico

Centuries ago, the Ancestral Puebloans left their mark on the area that would become New Mexico. They carved images into the volcanic rocks there, chipping away the top layers to create images of animals such as birds and serpents, people, geometric patterns, and more. Most were carved between 400 to 700 years ago, although some are believed to date back thousands of years. As the Spanish settlers arrived in the area, they too left their mark. In 1973, a section of the current national monument was set aside as Indian Petroglyph State Park. In 1990, Petroglyph National Monument was established to preserve more than 25,000 images.

There are multiple units at the monument, including Boca Negra Canyon. Boca Negra Canyon is popular for its developed trails.

Some petroglyphs are easily identified, but others are more difficult to decipher and understand.

The monument spans about 7,500 acres.

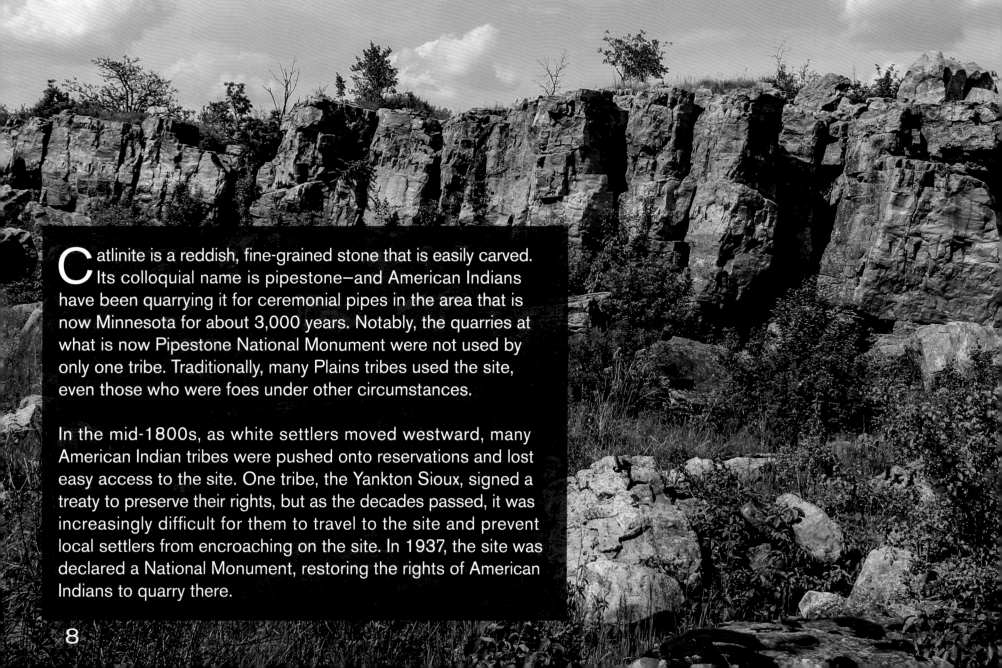

Pipestone National Monument
Pipestone County, Minnesota

Catlinite is a reddish, fine-grained stone that is easily carved. Its colloquial name is pipestone—and American Indians have been quarrying it for ceremonial pipes in the area that is now Minnesota for about 3,000 years. Notably, the quarries at what is now Pipestone National Monument were not used by only one tribe. Traditionally, many Plains tribes used the site, even those who were foes under other circumstances.

In the mid-1800s, as white settlers moved westward, many American Indian tribes were pushed onto reservations and lost easy access to the site. One tribe, the Yankton Sioux, signed a treaty to preserve their rights, but as the decades passed, it was increasingly difficult for them to travel to the site and prevent local settlers from encroaching on the site. In 1937, the site was declared a National Monument, restoring the rights of American Indians to quarry there.

The pipestone is surrounded by hard Sioux Quartzite. Hematite gives the rocks their reddish tint.

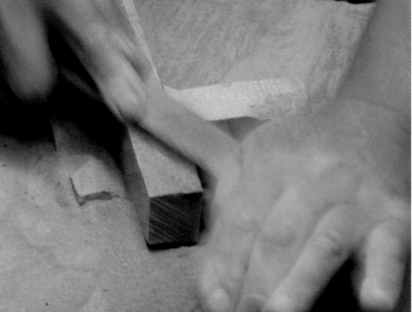

An active quarry site

Visitors to the monument can see demonstrations.

Pompeys Pillar
Yellowstone County, Montana

In 1806, after Meriwether Lewis and William Clark reached the Pacific Ocean, the duo decided to continue their exploration on their journey back east. In Montana, the explorers split their party into two groups, with Lewis heading off to the Blackfoot River, and Clark leading his group towards the Yellowstone River.

Just outside of Billings, Clark's expedition discovered a 150-foot tall rocky outcropping on the banks of the river. Clark climbed to the top and proclaimed he "had a most extensive view in every direction." Today, Pompeys Pillar National Monument is the location of the only known physical evidence of the Lewis and Clark Expedition. Clearly inscribed in the stone is William Clark's signature, left behind after his party—which included Sacagawea and her young son—explored the area. Clark himself dubbed the formation "Pompeys Pillar," in honor of Sacagawea's son. The boy, whose given name was Jean Baptiste Charbonneau, was playfully nicknamed "Pomp" or "Pompy."

William Clark's signature, which is dated July 25, 1806, isn't the only carving in the rock formation. The monument features many Native American petroglyphs, hundreds of initials left behind by early pioneers, and animal drawings. Experts believe some of the carvings date back 11,000 years!

The site was originally a part of the Crow Indian Reservation, and was purchased by the Foote family in 1955. But rising insurance costs forced the family to sell the land to the Bureau of Land Management, who formed an action group to preserve the site. The monument was designated a National Historic Landmark in 1965, and was officially named a National Monument on January 17, 2001.

Liberty Bell
Philadelphia, Pennsylvania

The inscription reads: Proclaim LIBERTY throughout all the Land unto all the Inhabitants thereof Lev. XXV v. X By Order of the ASSEMBLY of the Province of PENSYLVANIA [sic] for the State House in Philada

Pass and Stow
Philada
MDCCLIII

Americans today associate the Liberty Bell with the Revolutionary War, but as the inscription indicates, it was cast much earlier, in the 1750s, by John Pass and John Stow, for the Pennsylvania State House. There are records of abolitionists calling it Liberty Bell because of the engraved quote from Leviticus 25:10, but not until the 1830s. The bell didn't become popularly known as the Liberty Bell, and associated with the Revolutionary War, until decades after the fact. In 1847, a man named George Lippard wrote a popular story that described the bell ringing on July 4, 1776. Was there truth to the story? Historians think not. The bell could very well have been one of the bells that were rung when the Declaration of Independence was read on July 8th , but there's no contemporary record of that.

After the Civil War, however, the bell became an important symbol of national unity. An exhibition brought it around the country.

Today, Liberty Bell is part of Independence National Historical Park. The old Pennsylvania State House, also found on the site, is now Independence Hall.

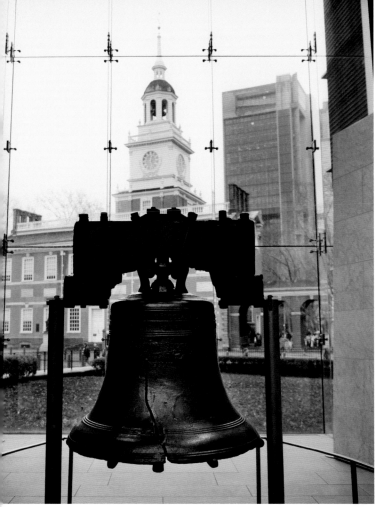

The cracks in the bell developed in the 1800s, likely the 1840s. In 1846, the decision was made to try widening the crack in order to restore the sound of the bell and stabilize the crack. Another crack, however, developed.

(Right) An 1885 cartoon illustrates the Liberty Bell being exhibited in New Orleans post-Civil War.

George Lippard *(right)* wrote the story "The Fourth of July, 1776," or "Ring, Grandfather, Ring," which popularized the idea that the bell rang on July 4, 1776.

(Left) The Liberty Bell returns home after the 1905 World's Fair in St. Louis.

Bunker Hill National Monument
Charlestown, Massachusetts

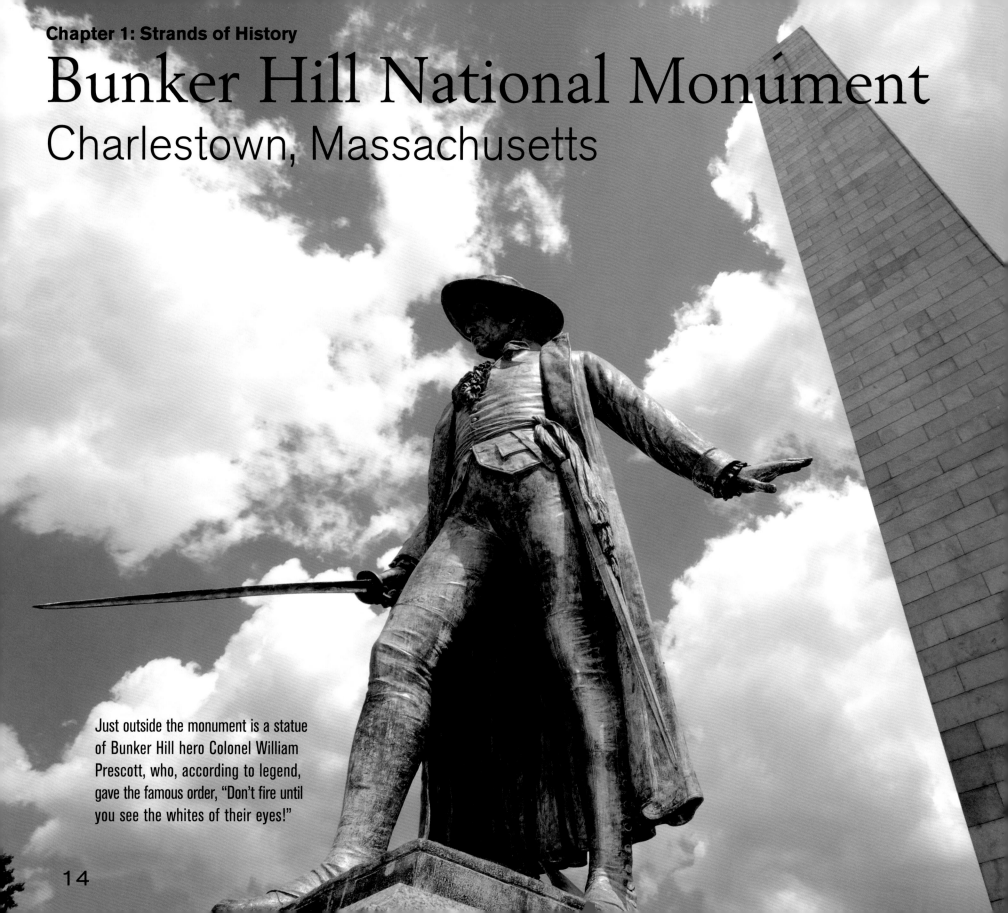

Just outside the monument is a statue of Bunker Hill hero Colonel William Prescott, who, according to legend, gave the famous order, "Don't fire until you see the whites of their eyes!"

THE BATTLE AT BUNKER'S HILL NEAR BOSTON.
June 17, 1775.

In the early morning hours of June 17, 1775, soldiers from Massachusetts, Connecticut, and New Hampshire hastily constructed a fort atop Breed's Hill, an area overlooking the settlement of Charlestown in Boston. By afternoon, British forces stormed the area, and the first major battle of the Revolutionary War was underway. Although most of the fighting took place at Breed's Hill, the confusion and hastiness of the battle led to a slight geographical mix-up, and the battle was named for the higher hill behind Breed's Hill: Bunker Hill.

The Bunker Hill Monument now stands on Breed's Hill to commemorate the famous Battle of Bunker Hill. The 221-foot tall granite obelisk was one of the first monuments in the United States, and was dedicated on June 17, 1843.

(Left) This 1834 print shows the Battle of Bunker Hill.

The cornerstone for the monument was laid in 1825 on the 50th anniversary of the battle. The stone was placed by Revolutionary War hero Marquis De Lafayette, who was a close friend of George Washington, Thomas Jefferson, and Alexander Hamilton.

Construction was halted on the obelisk several times due to a lack of funds. Because of this, it took seventeen years to complete the monument, with the capstone finally placed on July 23, 1842. This 1846 watercolor *(left)* shows the monument at the time.

Liberty Enlightening the World
New York City, New York

Ask any tourist in New York City which sites are on their list of must-sees, and no doubt the Statue of Liberty is one of them. In fact, about 4 million people visit the monument, which proudly stands on Liberty Island in New York Harbor, every year.

A gift from France to the United States, the statue was designed by Frederic Auguste Bartholdi, who was awarded a U.S. patent for his design in 1879. The monument was built by famed Eiffel Tower engineer Gustave Eiffel, and was officially dedicated on October 28, 1886.

The robed statue carries a torch in her right hand and a tablet in her left, and a broken chain lies at her feet. Representing Libertas, the Roman goddess of liberty, the monument is seen throughout the world as a symbol of freedom.

The outer layer of the statue is covered with copper that is only 3/32 of an inch thick. It was originally brownish in color, but over time, the now-familiar green patina developed due to the natural weathering of the copper.

Although access to the torch balcony has been restricted for safety reasons since 1916, visitors can still reserve tickets to climb to the crown. The ascension from the lobby to the crown is a total of 377 steps.

(Left) The tablet in the statue's left arm is inscribed with "JULY IV MDCCLXXVI." These are Roman numerals for July 4, 1776, the date of the Declaration of Independence.

While France gifted the statue itself, the United States funded the land and pedestal on which the statue rests. At one point, work on the pedestal was almost forced to stop when the money ran out, but famed publisher Joseph Pulitzer started a fundraiser to finance the construction. More than 120,000 people contributed, and the project was saved.

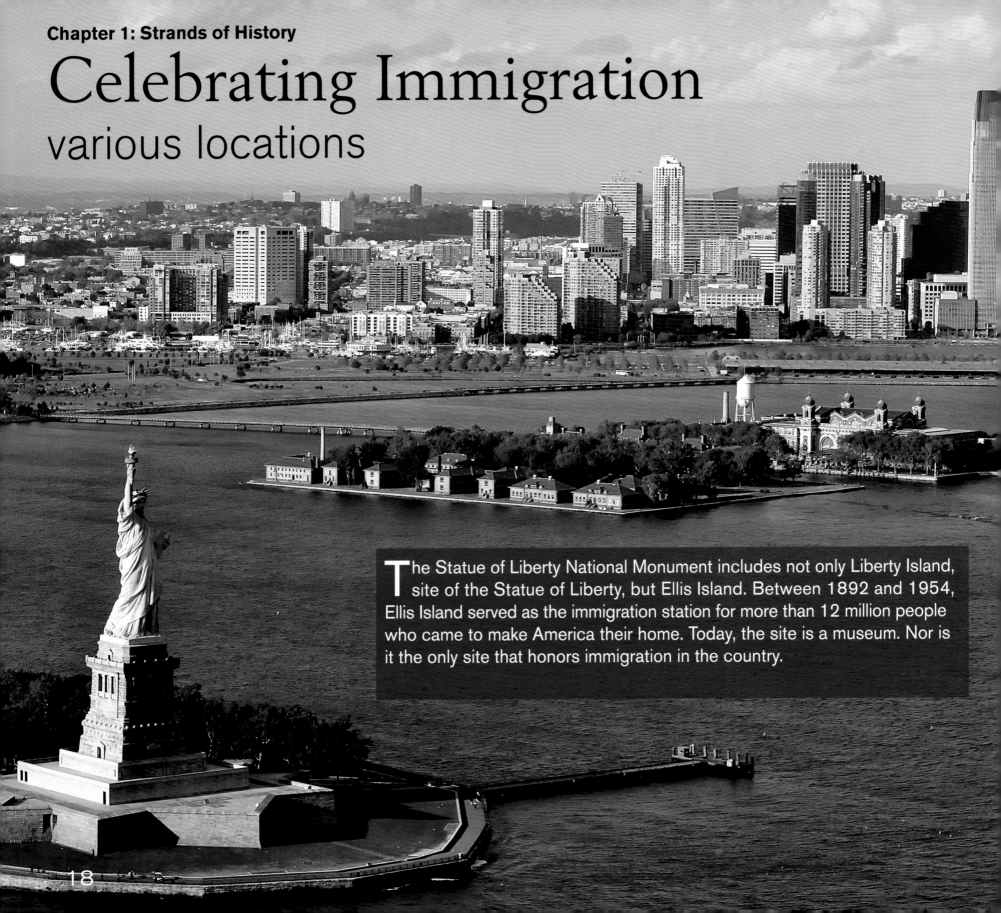

Celebrating Immigration
various locations

The Statue of Liberty National Monument includes not only Liberty Island, site of the Statue of Liberty, but Ellis Island. Between 1892 and 1954, Ellis Island served as the immigration station for more than 12 million people who came to make America their home. Today, the site is a museum. Nor is it the only site that honors immigration in the country.

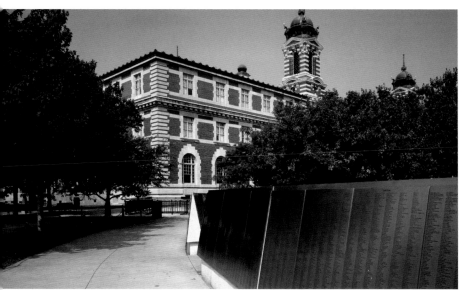

The Wall of Honor at Ellis Island lists more than 700,000 names. Families can honor their immigrant ancestors by having their names added to the Wall.

The Immigrants, cast by Luis Sanguino, is found in Battery Park in New York City. Its inscription reads: "DEDICATED TO THE PEOPLE OF ALL NATIONS / WHO ENTERED AMERICA THROUGH CASTLE GARDEN / IN MEMORY OF SAMUEL RUDIN / 1896-1975 / WHOSE PARENTS ARRIVED IN AMERICA IN 1883"

(Left) This monument from Wilmington, Delaware, is located at Fort Christina, the site of the first Swedish settlement in the United States in 1638.

Monument to the Immigrant was commissioned by the Italian-American Marching Club and sculpted by Franco Alessandrini. It is found in New Orleans, Louisiana.

Hermann Heights
New Ulm, Minnesota

At 32 feet tall, the figure of Hermann is one of the largest copper-plated statues in the United States. The height of the monument from foundation to sword tip is more than 100 feet.

In the year 9 C.E., a group of German tribes led by a chieftain named Arminius delivered a stinging defeat to the Roman army. So what does a German chieftain have to do with Minnesota? The memory of Arminius, later called Hermann, became important during the period when Germany became a unified nation in 1871. Between 1838 and 1875, a monument was built to honor Hermann and German heritage near the city of Detmold, Germany. Members of the German immigrant community in New Ulm, Minnesota, built a similar statue in their own community. The cornerstone was set in 1888 and the monument finished in 1897. In 2000, the U.S. Congress declared the monument to be a symbol of German-American heritage that recognized the contributions of German-American immigrants throughout the country.

This statue from Detmold, Germany, inspired its American counterpart.

Joan of Arc
New Orleans, Louisiana

The historical Joan of Arc was called the "Maid of Orléans" for her defense of that city from the English during the Hundred Years War. She died in 1431, burned at the stake, but her memory lives on in New Orleans in the form of a gilded monument. A relatively recent addition to the city, the statue was brought to the United States in 1958, where it spent some time in storage for financial reasons. It was finally placed in 1972, and then later moved to its current location on Decatur Street in the city's French Quarter.

The monument, which shows Joan of Arc riding on horseback with two cannons set in front of her, was a gift from the French people, and echoes a statue found in Paris. It celebrates the French heritage of Louisiana.

Little Bighorn Battlefield National Monument
Big Horn County, Montana

Located in southeastern Montana, the Little Bighorn Battlefield National Monument was created to remember the site of its namesake battle, which took place on June 25 and 26, 1876. Famously dubbed "Custer's Last Stand," the battle was waged between the 7th Cavalry Regiment of the United States Army, led by Lieutenant Colonel George Armstrong Custer, and the Lakota, Cheyenne, and Arapaho tribes, led by warriors including Crazy Horse and Chief Gall.

The first memorial on the site was created by Army officer George K. Sanderson in 1879, several years after Custer's defeat. In 1881, the remains of men who died at the site were interred in a mass grave—known as Last Stand Hill—and a granite memorial was added to mark the location. Starting on Memorial Day 1999, red granite markers have been added over the years to honor the Native Americans who fought in the battle.

In 1996, the National Park Service, along with members of the Indian nations who were a part of the battle, conducted a competition to create an Indian memorial for the battlefield. The winners were Philadelphia-based designers John R. Collins and Alison J. Towers, whose design is now displayed to honor the Native Americans who fought to preserve their way of life.

The site was originally known as Custer Battlefield National Monument, but in 1991, President George H.W. Bush signed a law to rename the site the Little Bighorn Battlefield National Monument.

Adjacent to the battlefield is Custer National Cemetery, which includes the graves of U.S. military veterans. It does not, however, include Custer himself, who was removed from the battlefield in 1877 and reinterred at West Point Cemetery.

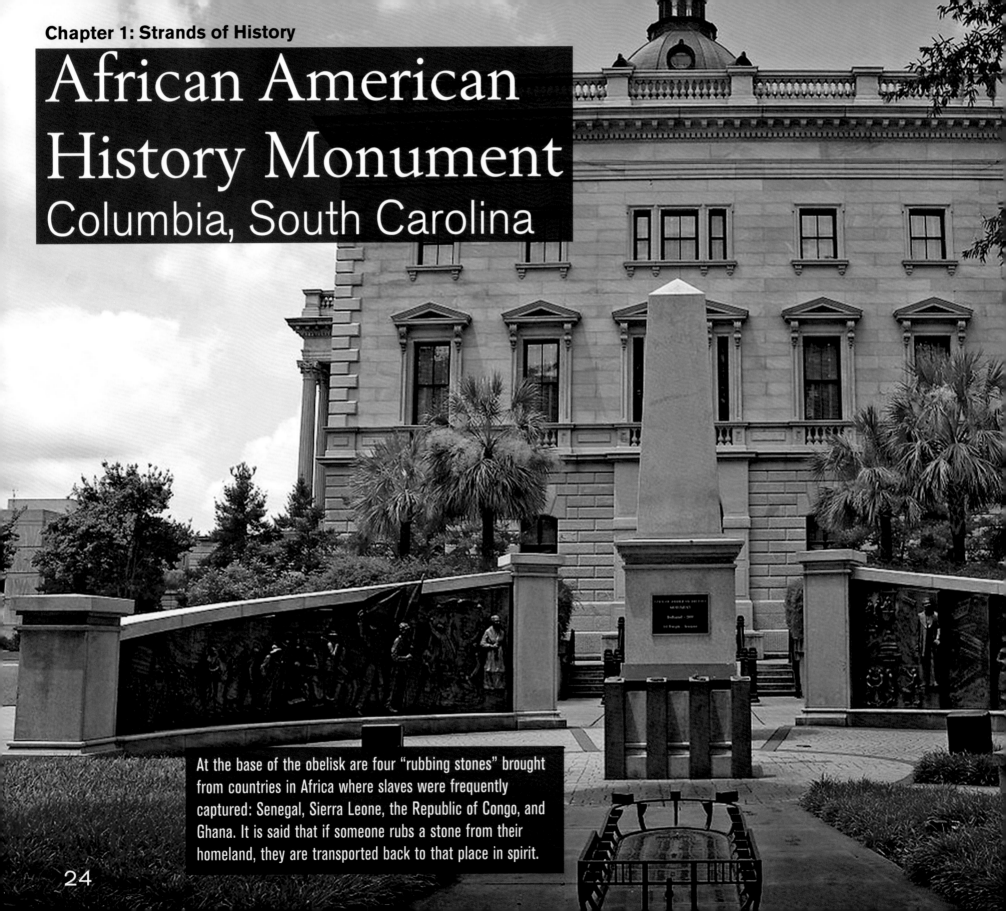

African American History Monument
Columbia, South Carolina

At the base of the obelisk are four "rubbing stones" brought from countries in Africa where slaves were frequently captured: Senegal, Sierra Leone, the Republic of Congo, and Ghana. It is said that if someone rubs a stone from their homeland, they are transported back to that place in spirit.

Dedicated on March 29, 2001, the African American History Monument is located on the grounds of the South Carolina capitol building in Columbia. Designed by Colorado sculptor Ed Dwight—who also created the Texas African American Historical Memorial in Austin, the Dr. Martin Luther King Jr. monument in Denver, and many other memorials celebrating black history—the monument depicts the history of African Americans in South Carolina.

Dwight designed the monument in a half-moon shape, to capture the feeling of an African village built in the round. The figures sculpted into granite on the two side panels tell the story of African Americans in South Carolina, from the 1619 slave auction blocks in Charleston to modern times. The centerpiece of the monument is a 22-foot tall granite obelisk, and a map of the "middle passage," through which millions of Africans sailed as part of the Atlantic slave trade.

Although the monument features 12 scenes that depict important moments in South Carolina history, no specific person is featured. This was done on purpose, to avoid any controversy or the appearance of favoritism.

The Keeper of the Plains
Wichita, Kansas

At the place where the Arkansas and Little Arkansas rivers meet, a 44-foot-tall statue stands proudly atop a 30-foot pedestal. Called *The Keeper of the Plains* and designed by Kiowa-Comanche sculptor Blackbear Bosin, the statue depicts an American Indian chief. It was commissioned to celebrate the United States Bicentennial and erected in 1974. A "Ring of Fire" surrounds the statue—fire pits that are lit for a period at night as the weather permits.

Dignity
Chamberlain, South Dakota

In September 2016, Dale Lamphere's sculpture *Dignity* was erected at a site overlooking the Missouri River, honoring both the state's 125th anniversary and the Dakota and Lakota peoples of the area. 50 feet tall, the sculpture depicts an Indigenous woman holding a star quilt. As the wind ripples over the blue patterns of the quilt, the stars shimmer in response.

In 2017, special license plates showing the figure of *Dignity* became available in South Dakota.

The Bennington Battle Monument

Bennington, Vermont

From the observation deck of this towering 306-foot obelisk, visitors can gaze out on three states: Vermont, Massachusetts, and New York. On August 16, 1777, during the Revolutionary War, militia forces from the fledgling U.S. and the Vermont Republic delivered a resounding defeat to British forces at what became known as the Battle of Bennington. The battle actually took place 10 miles away from Bennington in neighboring Walloomsac, New York. A century later, Vermonters began to plan a monument to memorialize the victory. Begun in 1887, the monument was completed in 1889, becoming and remaining the tallest structure in Vermont.

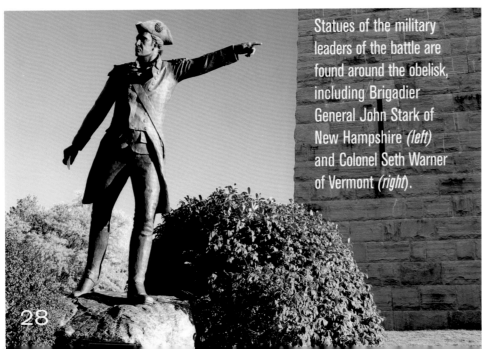

Statues of the military leaders of the battle are found around the obelisk, including Brigadier General John Stark of New Hampshire *(left)* and Colonel Seth Warner of Vermont *(right)*.

COL. SETH WARNER

SAVANNAH 9 OCT. 1779

(Left) General Casimir Pulaski, a Polish nobleman who fought for the Continental Army, died in battle in Savannah, Georgia. This monument marks his grave.

(Right) This statue of the Marquis de Lafayette is found in Lafayette Park, Washington, DC.

Other Revolutionary War Memorials

(Left) Like Lafayette, General Comte de Rochambeau was a Frenchman who fought in the Continental Army. He is honored here in Newport, Rhode Island.

(Right) This Carlisle, Pennsylvania, statue marks the grave of Molly Pitcher, Revolutionary War heroine of the Battle of Monmouth.

Perry's Victory and International Peace Memorial
Put-in-Bay, Ohio

Who was Perry and what did he win? If you live near the Erie Canal, know your naval history, or love studying the War of 1812, you may be familiar with Commodore Oliver Hazard Perry. During the War of 1812, he led U.S. naval forces against the British during the Battle of Lake Erie in September 1813. His victory over those forces helped American troops gain control of the lake. A hundred years after the war, the 352-foot monument was constructed, to remember not only the victory but to celebrate the long-standing peace between Britain, Canada, and the United States that followed. The flags of all three countries are flown at the site.

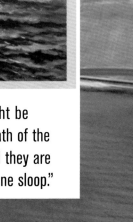

Even if you don't know Oliver Perry, you might be familiar with something he said. In the aftermath of the battle, he wrote: "We have met the enemy and they are ours. Two ships, two brigs, one schooner and one sloop."

Time *(also known as The Fountain of Time)*
Chicago, Illinois

The sculpture is carved out of concrete, as marble proved too expensive.

Renowned sculptor Lorado Taft *(see page 100)* created this massive monument found in Chicago's Washington Park. The sculpture shows Father Time presiding over 100 human figures in various stages of life, and commemorated the first 100 years of peace between the United States and Great Britain after the War of 1812. Water began running in the fountain in 1920, which was dedicated in 1922.

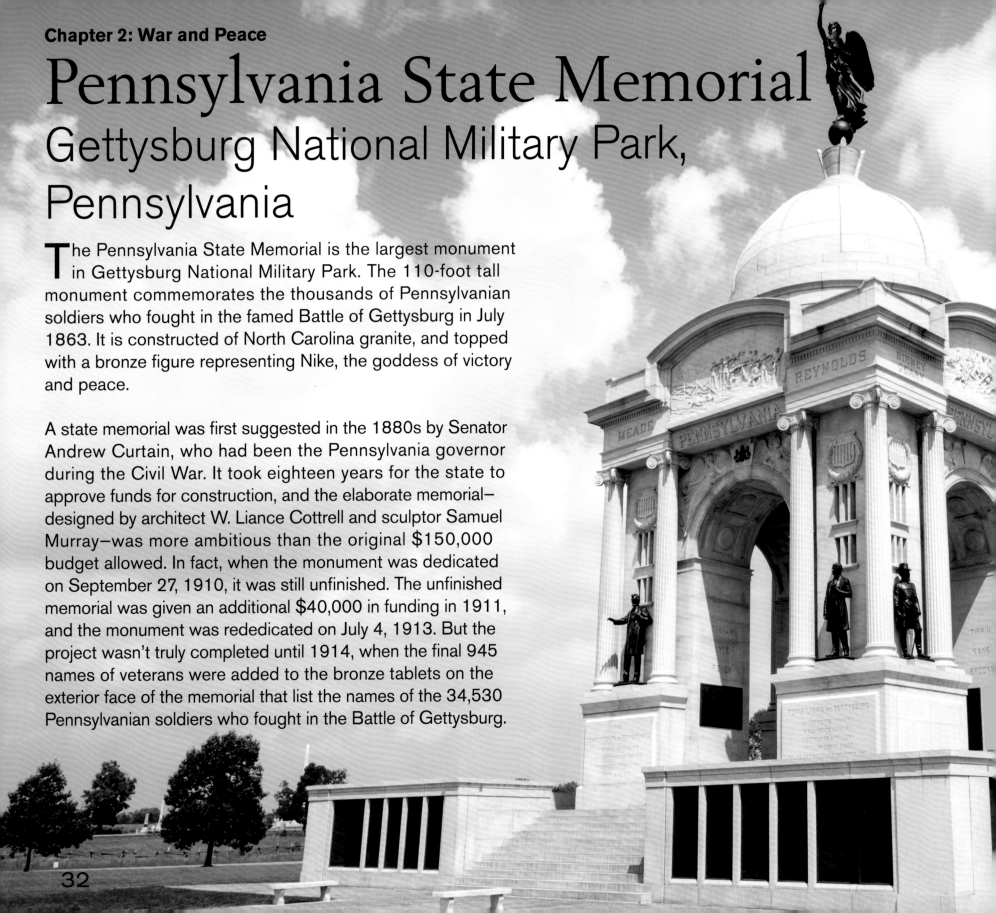

Pennsylvania State Memorial
Gettysburg National Military Park, Pennsylvania

The Pennsylvania State Memorial is the largest monument in Gettysburg National Military Park. The 110-foot tall monument commemorates the thousands of Pennsylvanian soldiers who fought in the famed Battle of Gettysburg in July 1863. It is constructed of North Carolina granite, and topped with a bronze figure representing Nike, the goddess of victory and peace.

A state memorial was first suggested in the 1880s by Senator Andrew Curtain, who had been the Pennsylvania governor during the Civil War. It took eighteen years for the state to approve funds for construction, and the elaborate memorial—designed by architect W. Liance Cottrell and sculptor Samuel Murray—was more ambitious than the original $150,000 budget allowed. In fact, when the monument was dedicated on September 27, 1910, it was still unfinished. The unfinished memorial was given an additional $40,000 in funding in 1911, and the monument was rededicated on July 4, 1913. But the project wasn't truly completed until 1914, when the final 945 names of veterans were added to the bronze tablets on the exterior face of the memorial that list the names of the 34,530 Pennsylvanian soldiers who fought in the Battle of Gettysburg.

The metal used to create the statue of Nike on top of the monument was reclaimed from melted-down Civil War cannons.

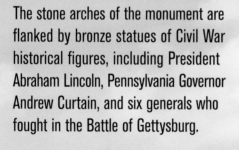

The stone arches of the monument are flanked by bronze statues of Civil War historical figures, including President Abraham Lincoln, Pennsylvania Governor Andrew Curtain, and six generals who fought in the Battle of Gettysburg.

Gettysburg National Military Park and the surrounding area are home to many other monuments to both Union and Confederate leaders, states, specific units, and individual soldiers.

Dedicated to Lincoln's famous address

To Arkansas soldiers

To Father William Corby, a Union Army chaplain. Indiana residents may be familiar with Corby, who later served as President of the University of Notre Dame in South Bend.

33

The Hiker
multiple locations

The name of the statue is *The Hiker*, but it doesn't celebrate enthusiastic nature lovers. Instead, it remembers battle-hardened soldiers who fought and died in the various military actions that took place between 1898 and 1902: the Spanish-American War, the Boxer Rebellion, and the Philippine-American War. Those soldiers called themselves "hikers," and sculptor Theo Alice Ruggles Kitson's work echoed the term. The original version of the statue was erected in 1906 in front of the armory at the University of Minnesota. In the 1920s, a company bought the reproduction rights and created another 50 replicas that are found scattered throughout the United States from Rhode Island to California.

Austin, Texas

Montgomery, Alabama

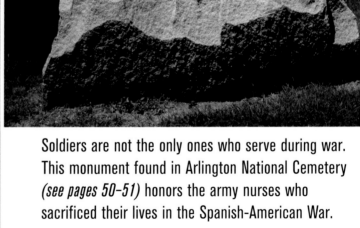

Soldiers are not the only ones who serve during war. This monument found in Arlington National Cemetery *(see pages 50–51)* honors the army nurses who sacrificed their lives in the Spanish-American War.

Winged Victory
Olympia, Washington

The inscription on one face of the *Winged Victory* monument reads, "To the memory of the citizens of the State of Washington who lost their lives in the service of the United States during the World War 1917 – 1918." Five figures are depicted: a soldier, a sailor, a marine, and a nurse, all shepherded by the Greek goddess Nike, who personified victory. Although a monument was first proposed in 1918, it took until 1927 before this monument was approved to go forward. It was dedicated on Memorial Day in 1938.

Inscriptions on the other faces of the monument read, "Greater love hath no man than this, that a man lay down his life for his friend," "Their sacrifice was to vindicate the principles of peace and justice in the life of the world," and "They fought to safeguard and transmit to posterity the principles of justice, freedom, and democracy."

National World War I Museum and Memorial
Kansas City, Missouri

A year after World War I ended in 1918, a group of Kansas City residents formed what they called the Liberty Memorial Association, or LMA. The LMA spearheaded efforts to create a memorial in honor of those who served in the war, and the group quickly raised an impressive $2.5 million for the project. The enthusiasm towards the memorial continued to the groundbreaking ceremony in 1921, where more than 100,000 people gathered, including then-Vice President Calvin Coolidge and five supreme Allied commanders who fought in the war.

Originally known as the Liberty Memorial, the monument was dedicated in 1926 by President Coolidge, who called it "one of the most elaborate and impressive memorials that adorn our country." By 1994, however, the structure had deteriorated to the point that it was forced to close. Once again, the people of Kansas City rallied to its aid, and with the help of federal and state government and individual donors, $102 million was raised to fund a revitalization project.

In 2004, Congress designated the Liberty Memorial the nation's official World War I museum. In 2006, it was named a National Historic Landmark. And in 2014, it was given a second designation to officially recognize it as the National World War I Museum and Memorial.

(Above) This image shows the 1921 dedication. The $2.5 million raised for the memorial in 1919 would be equivalent to around $34 million today!

The 217-foot Liberty Tower stands in the courtyard of the memorial, and can be ascended by elevator and 45 steps to an observation deck. At night, the tower emits steam and is lit with red and orange lights, to give the appearance of a flame.

To enter the main gallery, visitors cross a glass bridge over a field of 9,000 red poppies. Each poppy represents 1,000 lives lost, in remembrance of the 9 million lives lost in the war.

National World War II Memorial
Washington, D.C.

Forty-two years after the end of World War II, veteran Roger Durbin asked his state representative if a memorial could be constructed in honor of those who served in the second world war. It took another 17 years before Durbin's wish became a reality, and the National World War II Memorial was dedicated on May 29, 2004.

Located on the National Mall in Washington, D.C., the memorial was granted a prominent location between the Washington Monument to the east and the Lincoln Memorial to the west. Fifty-six 17-foot-tall granite pillars surround the memorial, with arches representing the Atlantic and the Pacific on either end.

Sadly, Roger Durbin, the man who sparked interest in the memorial, passed away two years before it was completed. A History Channel documentary about the construction of the memorial was dedicated in his honor.

The addition of the monument on the National Mall marked the first time in 70 years that a memorial was placed in the corridor between the Capitol and the Potomac River.

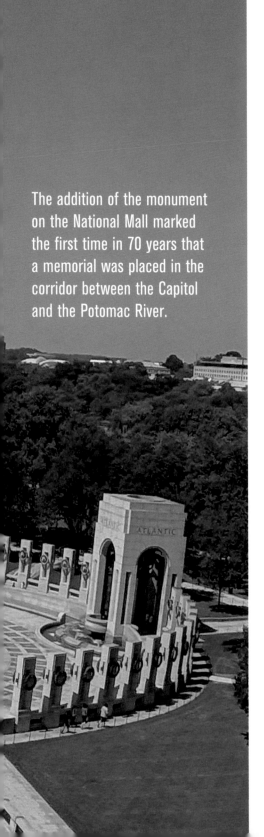

The 56 pillars surrounding the memorial represent the 48 states that were part of the U.S. in 1945, plus the Alaska and Hawaii territories, the District of Columbia, the Commonwealth of the Philippines, Puerto Rico, Guam, American Samoa, and the U.S. Virgin Islands.

The memorial features bas-relief artwork depicting important moments in the war, including D-Day, the Battle of the Bulge, and Pearl Harbor.

Keen observers can find two "Kilroy was here" engravings placed in nondescript areas of the memorial. World War II soldiers used to leave "Kilroy was here" graffiti at locations they were stationed or visited.

USS *Arizona* Memorial
Pearl Harbor, Honolulu, Hawaii

On December 7, 1941, the United States was caught off guard by an attack on the naval base at Pearl Harbor in Honolulu, Hawaii. Japanese planes bombed "battleship row," where ships including the USS *Tennessee*, USS *Oklahoma*, and USS *California* were heavily damaged. Hit hardest was the USS *Arizona*, which sustained irreparable damage and sunk to the bottom of the harbor. Of the 2,403 people who lost their lives that day, 1,177 of them were on the USS *Arizona*.

In 1958, President Eisenhower approved the construction of a national memorial for the site, and the USS *Arizona* Memorial—accessible only by boat—was constructed over the sunken remains of the ship. It was dedicated on May 30, 1962, and is jointly administered by the U.S. Navy and the National Park Service. Today, the USS *Arizona* still rests where she fell, a memorial not only for its crewmembers, but for all who gave their lives that day.

The USS *Missouri* is found near the USS *Arizona* Memorial. On this ship, General Douglas MacArthur and Admiral Chester Nimitz accepted Japanese surrender. This view from the deck of the USS *Missouri* shows the USS *Arizona* Memorial in the distance.

The memorial's shape, which is raised on each end and bows in at the middle, is said to represent American pride before the war, the country's depression during the war, and rising American power after the war.

The USS *Arizona* was carrying around 1.5 million gallons of oil when she sunk, and the ship has continually leaked oil since then. Approximately two to nine quarts of oil leak from the ship every day, and oil slicks—known as the "tears of the Arizona"—can be observed from the memorial site.

ARIZONA BB 39

USS *Arizona* crewmembers who survived the attack are given the right to have their cremated remains interred inside the ship. After a funeral ceremony, National Park Service divers place the remains inside the barbette of gun turret four, so that sailors can rejoin their fallen shipmates. More than 40 surviving crewmembers have now been returned to the ship.

Manzanar National Historic Site
near Independence, California

During World War II, more than 100,000 Japanese Americans were incarcerated in ten relocation camps. One of those camps, holding about 10,000 people, was Manzanar. As a National Historic Site, it preserves the stories from that bleak chapter in American history. Visitors to the site can see reconstructed barracks and a replica guard tower, as well as Japanese gardens.

The obelisk shown here was erected in 1943 by the incarcarees to memorialize their dead. The inscription reads, "Monument to console the souls of the dead."

Noted landscape photographer Ansel Adams chronicled the experience of the incarcerees at Manzanar.

A wooden bridge in what was a Japanese garden

Origami decorations remember those who died at Manzanar.

This building is a reconstruction of one of the thirty-six residential blocks built to house families. Conditions were crowded and cramped.

43

Korean War Memorials

various locations

The Korean War has often been called "The Forgotten War" or "The Unknown War," as World War II and the Vietnam War, the conflicts that occurred before and after, garnered much more public attention. Monuments throughout the country, however, ensure that the service members who fought in the war will not be forgotten. The Korean War Veterans Memorial in Washington, D.C.'s West Potomac Park consists of a mural wall, 19 stainless steel statues depicting soldiers, and the Pool of Remembrance, where memorial attendees can sit beneath linden trees and reflect on their visit.

This monument to the Korean War, found in New York City's Battery Park, was dedicated in 1991. It honors not only U.S. military personnel but fighters from other countries including Australia, France, and the United Kingdom.

The Korean War Memorial in Atlantic City, New Jersey, was dedicated in 2000.

This monument to Korean War Veterans is found in Nashville, Tennessee.

This monument is found in Memphis, Tennessee. It is located in Veterans Plaza in Overton Park, along with other memorials.

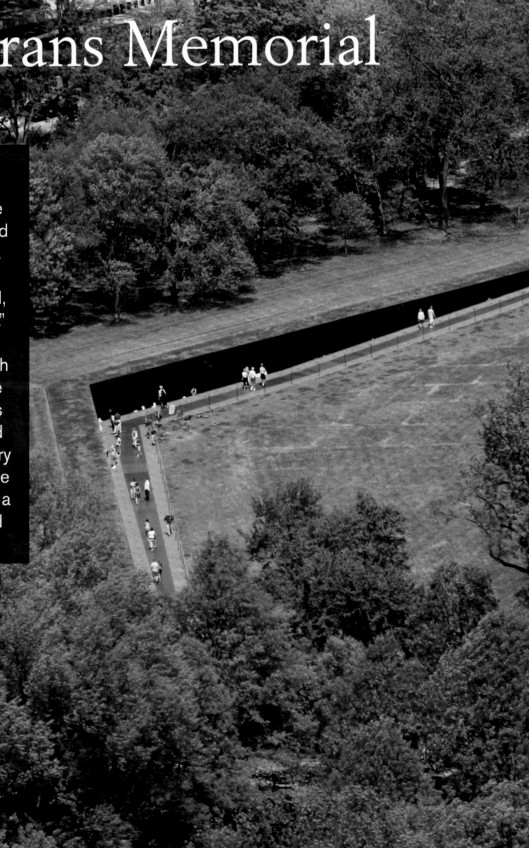

Vietnam Veterans Memorial
Washington, D.C.

As one of the most visited memorials in Washington, D.C.—second only to the Lincoln Memorial—it is surprising to learn that the Vietnam Veterans Memorial was not well received when it was dedicated on November 13, 1982. Artist Maya Lin's design was considered too unconventional and plain to be a war memorial, with one critic calling it a "black gash of shame."

The simple design consists of two walls, each 246-foot-9-inch long, which are sunk into the ground and meet together in a V shape. Lin's vision was to create a memorial that symbolized a healing wound, to reflect the pain and recovery the country experienced after the war. Today, the Vietnam Veterans Memorial is no longer seen as a "black gash of shame," but rather as a shrine and place of reflection and respect.

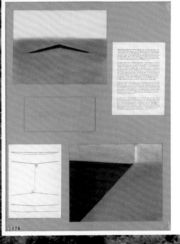

Maya Lin was only 21 years old when her design was chosen out of 1,441 submissions in a public design competition for the monument.

As a compromise to those who felt the memorial was too basic, a bronze sculpture–created by Frederick Hart–was added a short distance from the wall. Called *The Three Servicemen,* the traditionally styled sculpture features three soldiers who appear to gaze at the names of their fallen friends on the wall.

Visitors often leave items at the wall for sentimental reasons. More than 400,000 items have been left since the memorial's dedication. These have included everything from flags, medals, letters, and photos to cans of beer, roller skates, and even a motorcycle.

The Vietnam Woman's Memorial by Glenna Goodacre was dedicated in 1993.

Throughout the Country

Unconditional Surrender, based off the famous World War II photograph, was first installed in Sarasota in 2005. Other versions of the statue can be found in different locations.

An international monument, the Peace Arch stands on the border between Blaine, Washington, and British Columbia, Canada. It was built in 1921 to celebrate a century of peace between the two countries. Inscriptions read, "Children of a common mother" and "Brethren dwelling together in unity."

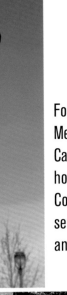

Found in Veterans Memorial Park in Napa, California, this sculpture honors those in Napa County who died while serving in Afghanistan and Iraq.

This Fairbanks, Alaska, monument honors pilots who flew along the Alaska-Siberia Lend Lease Airway during World War II.

Dedicated in 1977 to "Those Americans Lost in Southeast Asia Combat," the Missing Man Monument is found at Randolph Air Force base in San Antonio, Texas.

Monuments at Arlington National Cemetery
Arlington County, Virginia

Established in 1864, Arlington National Cemetery is the burial site for some 400,000 people: veterans of America's wars, and, in some cases, their family members. Perhaps the most familiar memorial is the Tomb of the Unknown Soldier, but there are many found throughout the site, including ones that honor chaplains, the military personnel who died while attempting a rescue of American hostages in Iran in 1980, those who fought in the Battle of the Bulge, those who died in the 1983 bombing of American Marines barracks in Beirut, those who died in the bombing of Pan Am Flight 103 in 1998, and the Rough Riders.

The inscription on the Tomb of the Unknown Soldier reads, "Here rests in honored glory an American soldier known but to God." It rests atop the grave of an unknown soldier from World War I.

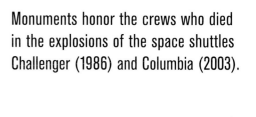

Monuments honor the crews who died in the explosions of the space shuttles Challenger (1986) and Columbia (2003).

A monument to Army and Navy nurses was unveiled in 1938, at the ceremony shown here.

This monument to the Coast Guard is shown in 1928, during its construction.

51

United States Marine Corps War Memorial
Arlington County, Virginia

One of the most iconic moments of World War II is captured in sculpture at the United States Marine Corps War Memorial. Sculptor Felix de Weldon used the famous photo of Marines raising a U.S. flag on Mount Suribachi as his inspiration for the statue, which is also commonly known as the Iwo Jima Memorial. The memorial honors not only those who lost their lives during WWII, but all Marines who have died serving the country since the Marine Corps began in 1775.

Commissioned in 1951, the memorial now sits outside Arlington National Cemetery. Architect Horace W. Pealee constructed the base for the statue out of granite from a quarry in Sweden. De Weldon first sculpted the 32-foot high figures in plaster, then disassembled them so they could be cast in bronze. Finally, the bronze pieces were trucked to Washington D.C. and welded together.

The base of the monument is engraved with the name and date of every major conflict since the beginning of the Corps.

In 1961, President John F. Kennedy declared that the U.S. flag should continually fly over the monument. Since then, the flag has flown 24 hours a day, 365 days a year on the 60-foot flagpole at the site.

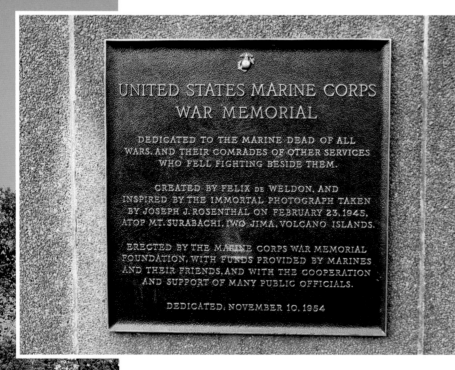

The memorial was dedicated on November 10, 1954, which was the 179th anniversary of the founding of the Marine Corps. President Dwight D. Eisenhower and Vice President Richard Nixon attended the ceremony.

Soldiers and Sailors
Indianapolis, Indiana

In the middle of Monument Circle, in the center of the city of Indianapolis, Indiana, rises the 284-foot Soldiers and Sailors Monument. The cornerstone was laid in 1889, with construction continuing until 1901 and the dedication taking place a year later. While it began as a Civil War monument, inscriptions on the monument honor veterans from the Revolutionary War, the War of 1812, and the Mexican-American War as well.

First cast in bronze in 1987 for the United States Navy Memorial, the Lone Sailor stands watch in more than a dozen locations throughout the country. You can see him in such diverse places as South Carolina's Charleston Naval Memorial Park, the Great Lakes Naval Training Center in Illinois, and in front of the USS *Wisconsin,* now serving as a museum ship in Virginia. This photograph shows the original statue in D.C.

The United States Air Force Memorial
Fort Myer, Arlington County, Virginia

Though the idea of a United States Air Force Memorial was first authorized in 1993, it took some time for this monument to get off the ground due to controversy over the site suggested. In 2002, James Ingo Freed's design, showing three spires reminiscent of contrails coming from Air Force Thunderbirds, was approved, and construction followed in short order. The monument was dedicated in 2006, with speaker George W. Bush promising, "To all who have climbed sunward and chased the shouting wind, America stops to say: your service and your sacrifice will be remembered forever, and honored in this place by the citizens of a free and grateful nation."

Zenos Frudakis sculpted the four figures of the Honor Guard.

First Responders

Numerous statues and monuments dedicated to police officers and firefighters are found throughout the country. These are just a few.

This statue of a police officer is found on the grounds of Alabama's State Capitol in Montgomery.

This monument to firefighters is found on the grounds of California's State Capitol.

DUTY CALLED

GREATER LOVE HATH NO MAN THAN THIS: "THAT HE GIVES HIS LIFE TO SAVE A FRIEND" LAW ENFORCEMENT OFFICERS DO EVEN MORE, SOMETIMES THEY GIVE THEIR LIVES TO SAVE A STRANGER.

BRANKO MEDENICA SCULPTOR

Found in New York City's Battery Park, this Police Memorial was dedicated in 1997.

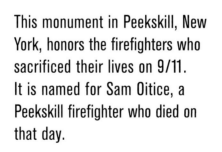

This monument in Peekskill, New York, honors the firefighters who sacrificed their lives on 9/11. It is named for Sam Oitice, a Peekskill firefighter who died on that day.

In One Moment
Duty became sacrifice
A flag became strength
A man became a memory

All in One Moment

Military and Working Dogs

various locations

Lyon, Michigan, is home to the Michigan War Dog Memorial Cemetery.

Monuments to human struggles and achievements have been constructed in this country for centuries. But what about our hard-working canine counterparts? Don't worry; they haven't been forgotten. There are multiple monuments and statues that pay homage to military and K9 dogs. There's even a national monument: the Military Working Dog Teams National Monument on Lackland Air Force Base in San Antonio, Texas, pays tribute to these often-unsung heroes. (Although the monument is on a secure Air Force base, the law requires that the Department of Defense provide the public was reasonable access to the monument. Visitors must request a base pass, and are allowed up to four hours to view the monument.)

Plymouth Rock
Plymouth, Massachusetts

In 1620, the Mayflower pilgrims landed in what became Massachusetts. Plymouth Rock marks their traditional landing site. Whether the rock was there at that point is an open question; contemporary documents do not refer to it. Throughout the years, the rock itself has been relocated multiple times. It's also become smaller, as pieces have been chipped off for souvenirs.

(Left) Tourists visit the Plymouth Rock site, protected by a pavilion.

(Above) The rock is engraved with the landing date.

National Monument to the Forefathers
Plymouth, Massachusetts

Plymouth Rock is part of Massachusetts's Pilgrim Memorial State Park. Another monument in that same park is the National Monument to the Forefathers. The cornerstone for this large granite statue was laid in 1859, with the completion and dedication taking place in 1888 and 1889. The names of the Mayflower pilgrims are inscribed on the monument, as are these words: "National Monument to the Forefathers. Erected by a grateful people in remembrance of their labors, sacrifices and sufferings for the cause of civil and religious liberty."

The figures shown are not those of the pilgrims, but allegorical figures: Faith, which brought the Pilgrims on their journey, stands on the main pedestal. She is surrounded by Morality, Law, Education, and Liberty.

Statues of Massasoit *(left)* and the Pilgrim Mothers *(right)* can also be found in Plymouth, Massachusetts. They date back to 1920–the time of the Tercentenary Celebration.

(Left) A 1900 photograph shows the monument about a decade after its dedication.

(Right) An 1876 Currier and Ives print shows an artist's conception of the Pilgrims at the time the monument was being built.

Sergeant Floyd Monument
Sioux City, Iowa

O ne of Kentucky's native sons is honored in Sioux City, Iowa, with a gleaming obelisk standing 100 feet tall. Charles Floyd acted as quartermaster for the Lewis and Clark expedition that began in 1804. He died in August of that year, probably from a ruptured appendix. Fortunately, he was the only fatality from the Corps of Discovery.

Floyd had kept a diary of his expedition experiences. In 1901, not long after an 1894 printing that sparked interest in his life and death, the current monument was raised.

Floyd is buried near the monument.

Sacagawea
various locations

The most famous member of the Lewis and Clark expedition after Lewis and Clark, Sacagawea was only a teenager when she took part in the expedition. A Lehmi Shoshone who had been captured by the Hidatsa, she served as interpreter for the expedition—and gave birth to Jean Baptiste Charbonneau. She has continually captured and recaptured the imagination of the public, serving as the namesake for various mountain peaks, rivers, and trails, especially in the Western states. She's also been the subject of numerous statues, some of which are shown here.

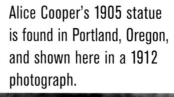

A statue found in Fort Clatsop, where the expedition wintered, now part of Lewis and Clark National Historical Park

Alice Cooper's 1905 statue is found in Portland, Oregon, and shown here in a 1912 photograph.

This statue is found in Bismarck, North Dakota.

Gateway Arch
St. Louis, Missouri

At 630 feet tall, the arch is the nation's tallest monument, the tallest man-made monument in the Western Hemisphere, the tallest accessible building in Missouri, and the tallest arch in the world!

The Gateway Arch, often called the St. Louis Arch, is the focal point of the Jefferson National Expansion Memorial. This park, located in St. Louis, Missouri, is situated near the starting point of the Lewis and Clark Expedition, and was designated a National Memorial in 1935.

The park was created in honor of Thomas Jefferson and what was considered one of his greatest achievements: the acquisition of the Louisiana territory in the Louisiana Purchase. The arch itself was created as a monument to western expansion in the United States. It was designed by Finnish-American architect Eero Saarinen in 1947, but construction was delayed until 1963 due to a lack of funding and disagreements about rerouting a railroad running near the site of the arch.

The arch was finally completed in 1965, was dedicated on May 25, 1968, and designated a National Historic Landmark in 1987.

The observation deck can hold 160 people, and features 32 windows which are only 7 by 27 inches. The small windows are necessary due to the immense pressure exerted by the two halves of the arch meeting together at the top.

A pessimistic actuarial firm predicted that thirteen workers would die while the arch was being built. Fortunately, they were wrong—not one worker lost their life during construction. This photo was taken during the construction process.

The top of the arch is accessible by two trams—one in each leg—that are made up of eight cylindrical, five-seat compartments. The compartments rotate as they travel up the arch, not unlike Ferris wheel cars. There are 1,076 emergency stairs located in each leg of the structure.

Madonna of the Trail
various locations

Springfield, Ohio. Wheeling, West Virginia. Council Grove, Kansas. Lexington, Missouri. Lamar, Colorado. Albuquerque, New Mexico. Springerville, Arizona. Vandalia, Illinois. Richmond, Indiana. Beallsville, Pennsylvania. Upland, California. Bethseda, Maryland.

What links these twelve geographically diverse locations? They were states that formed a cross-country route on the National Old Trails Road, established in 1912–and they all host statues showing a pioneering woman: the Madonna of the Trail. The drive behind the statues came from the National Society of the Daughters of the American Revolution, who commissioned sculptor August Leimbach and raised the money for the statues. The various statues were dedicated in 1928 and 1929.

The sculptor, a German immigrant, wrote, "When I came to America, I often saw these people of the pioneer type, strong and brave and always ready to protect themselves against any danger. Asked to make a sketch model for a monument of a woman of pioneer days, I was inspired by my own impression of these people I had met, and the Madonna of the Trail is the result."

Lamar, Colorado

MADONNA OF THE TRAIL

MADONNA OF THE TRAIL

BY THE AUTHORITY OF THE
UNITED STATES GOVERNMENT
AND CHIEFLY THROUGH
THE STATESMANSHIP OF
HENRY CLAY
THIS ROAD WAS MADE POSSIBLE
IN 1806

N·S·D·A·R· MEMORIAL
TO THE
PIONEER MOTHERS
OF THE
COVERED WAGON DAYS

Missouri judge and future U.S. president Harry Truman was the president of the National Old Trails Road Association during this time and attended several of the dedication ceremonies.

Wheeling, West Virginia

Great Platte River Road Archway
Kearney, Nebraska

D riving through Nebraska on I-80, drivers pass under the Great Platte River Road Archway. The Great Platte River Road has a long history: It was a route along several trails used by settlers, including the Oregon Trail. Kearney, Nebraska is located near Fort Kearny, which was a historic outpost on the Oregon Trail. The Archway, which opened to the public in July 2000, commemorates that history, with museum exhibits about the various trails and the sights pioneers would have seen. It also details the many years of transportation history that followed, from Pony Express Riders to the building of the transcontinental railroad to the construction of highways.

Other sites in Nebraska related to the Oregon Trail include Scotts Bluff National Monument *(top)* and Chimney Rock National Historical Site *(bottom)*. Both are natural geological formations that acted as landmarks to travelers.

Washington Monument
Washington, D.C.

As "the father of his country," it was almost inevitable that George Washington would be honored with a memorial in the nation's capital. In fact, talk of a monument in his honor began long before his death in 1799. But it would take nearly a century—until 1888—before his namesake monument was open to the public.

As early as 1783, proposals for a monument to the country's first president were considered. But disagreements over design and political power struggles served to delay construction. Finally, in 1848, the cornerstone was laid and work began on architect Robert Mills' obelisk design. Lack of funding and the onset of the Civil War halted construction once again, and it took another 36 years before the capstone was set in 1884. The monument was dedicated on February 21, 1885, and at last—on October 9, 1888—the Washington Monument was open, receiving an average of 55,000 visitors a month in its first year.

The east and west interior walls of the monument contain almost 200 commemorative stones, donated by cities, states, foreign governments, and various organizations. These include stones from all 50 states, college alumni associations, fire departments, and the countries of Japan, Turkey, and Brazil.

The monument is topped with a nine-inch pyramid of solid aluminum, which was considered a rare metal in the 1800s. At the time it was placed, it was the largest piece of aluminum in the world.

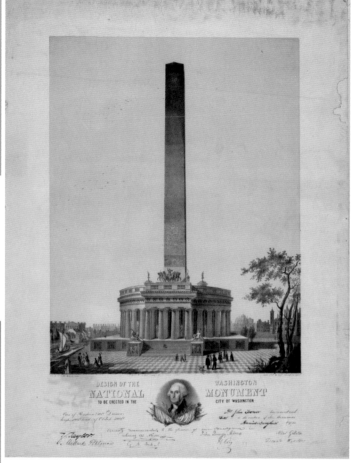

When the monument was completed, it was the world's tallest structure, at 555 feet. It held this title until 1889, when the Eiffel Tower surpassed it. This image from the 1840s shows Robert Mills' design.

A close look reveals that the stone used in the obelisk slightly changes color after the first 150 feet of the monument. This marks the location where construction stopped just before the Civil War. When it resumed, the marble used was from a different quarry, giving the monument a two-tone appearance.

Thomas Jefferson Memorial
Washington, D.C.

The memorial is bordered by some of Washington, D.C.'s famous blossoming cherry trees, which were a gift from the people of Japan in 1912.

In 1934, one of the country's most influential presidents, Franklin Delano Roosevelt, suggested that a memorial be built for another influential president he greatly admired: Thomas Jefferson. FDR felt that Jefferson, as the main drafter of the Declaration of Independence, first U.S. Secretary of State, and third U.S. president, deserved a monument of recognition. Congress agreed and appropriated $3 million for the project.

Construction began in 1938 in West Potomac Park on the shore of the Potomac River Tidal Basin. Jefferson himself was a fan of neoclassical architecture, and is often credited with introducing the design to the United States. So memorial designer John Russell Pope modeled the building after the Pantheon in Rome, with marble Ionic columns surrounding a circular colonnade. Inside stands a 19-foot-tall bronze statue of Jefferson, sculpted by Rudulph Evans, and excerpts from the Declaration of Independence adorn panels on the walls.

The Commission of Fine Arts, which reviews construction projects in Washington, D.C., never gave its approval for the memorial, and opposed its construction. But FDR gave the project permission to proceed anyway, despite the controversy.

The memorial was dedicated by President Roosevelt on April 13, 1943, which was the 200th anniversary of Jefferson's birthday. This 1939 photograph shows his presence at the laying of the cornerstone.

Sculptor Adolph A. Weinman created the relief positioned over the entrance to the memorial. It depicts five members of the Declaration of Independence drafting committee submitting their proposal to Congress.

Lincoln Memorial
Washington, D.C.

The path to the Lincoln Memorial began in 1867, very soon after Lincoln's death, when Congress introduced legislation forming a Lincoln Monument Association. That Association proposed a massive sculpture on the grounds of the Capitol. However, it was never built. In the decades that followed, other memorials were considered. Finally, in 1910, Congress approved the bill to allow the current memorial, and construction began a few years later. The memorial was dedicated in 1922.

The designer of the monument, architect Henry Bacon, was inspired by ancient Greek temples like the Parthenon. The sculpture of Lincoln was designed by Daniel Chester French and carved by the six Piccirilli brothers under French's direction. Jules Guerin created the murals "Emancipation" and "Unity," found inside the Memorial. Royal Cortissoz wrote the words found above Lincoln's statue.

In 1939, racial segregation was still practiced. Opera singer Marian Anderson, denied of the chance to perform at Constitution Hall because she was African American, delivered a concert at the Lincoln Memorial.

In 1963, Martin Luther King, Jr., delivered his "I have a dream" speech on the steps of the Lincoln Memorial. In 2003, forty years later, an inscription about that speech was added to the step on which King stood when he gave the speech.

As president, William Taft signed the 1911 bill to create the Memorial. In 1922, as Chief Justice, he dedicated the memorial.

Bacon incorporated different types of stone drawn from different parts of the Union. The memorial includes granite from Massachusetts, marble from Colorado, Tennessee, Georgia, and Alabama, and limestone from Indiana.

IN THIS TEMPLE
AS IN THE HEARTS OF THE PEOPLE
FOR WHOM HE SAVED THE UNION
THE MEMORY OF ABRAHAM LINCOLN
IS ENSHRINED FOREVER

FOUR SCORE AND SEVEN YEARS
AGO OUR FATHERS BROUGHT FORTH
ON THIS CONTINENT A NEW NATION
CONCEIVED IN LIBERTY AND DEDICA-
TED TO THE PROPOSITION THAT ALL
MEN ARE CREATED EQUAL ·
NOW WE ARE ENGAGED IN A GREAT
CIVIL WAR TESTING WHETHER THAT
NATION OR ANY NATION SO CON-
CEIVED AND SO DEDICATED CAN LONG
ENDURE · WE ARE MET ON A GREAT
BATTLEFIELD OF THAT WAR · WE HAVE
COME TO DEDICATE A PORTION OF
THAT FIELD AS A FINAL RESTING
PLACE FOR THOSE WHO HERE GAVE
THEIR LIVES THAT THAT NATION
MIGHT LIVE · IT IS ALTOGETHER FIT-
TING AND PROPER THAT WE SHOULD
DO THIS · BUT IN A LARGER SENSE
WE CAN NOT DEDICATE-WE CAN NOT
CONSECRATE-WE CAN NOT HALLOW-
THIS GROUND · THE BRAVE MEN LIV-
ING AND DEAD WHO STRUGGLED HERE
HAVE CONSECRATED IT FAR ABOVE
OUR POOR POWER TO ADD OR DETRACT·
THE WORLD WILL LITTLE NOTE NOR
LONG REMEMBER WHAT WE SAY HERE
BUT IT CAN NEVER FORGET WHAT THEY
DID HERE · IT IS FOR US THE LIVING
RATHER TO BE DEDICATED HERE TO
THE UNFINISHED WORK WHICH THEY
WHO FOUGHT HERE HAVE THUS FAR
SO NOBLY ADVANCED · IT IS RATHER FOR
US TO BE HERE DEDICATED TO THE
GREAT TASK REMAINING BEFORE US-
THAT FROM THESE HONORED DEAD
WE TAKE INCREASED DEVOTION TO
THAT CAUSE FOR WHICH THEY GAVE THE
LAST FULL MEASURE OF DEVOTION-
THAT WE HERE HIGHLY RESOLVE THAT
THESE DEAD SHALL NOT HAVE DIED IN
VAIN-THAT THIS NATION UNDER GOD
SHALL HAVE A NEW BIRTH OF FREEDOM-
AND THAT GOVERNMENT OF THE PEOPLE
BY THE PEOPLE FOR THE PEOPLE SHALL
NOT PERISH FROM THE EARTH ·

Two speeches are inscribed in the chambers of the memorial: the Gettysburg Address and Lincoln's Second Inaugural Address.

MONTANA   WASHINGTON   IDAHO   WYOMING   UTAH   OKLAHOMA   NEW
MDCCCLXXXIX   MDCCCLXXXIX   MDCCCXC   MDCCCXC   MDCCCXCVI   MCMVII

VERMONT   KENTUCKY   TENNESSEE
MDCCXCI   MDCCXCII   MDCCXCVI

The 36 columns that surround the monument represent the 36 states that comprised the Union when Lincoln was assassinated in 1865.

Ulysses S. Grant Memorial
Washington, D.C.

One of the largest equestrian statues in the world honors Ulysses S. Grant, general and president. Appropriately enough for this Civil War general, it is found in Union Square.

The memorial consists of three parts. At the center of the monument stands the equestrian statue of Grant, surrounding by lions. At either side, there are sculptures showing soldiers in action: *Artillery* and *Cavalry Charge.*

The impetus for the monument came from Civil War veterans in the Army of the Tennessee. Congress approved the funding in 1901, and a search for architects and a design commenced. In the years that followed, the lions, the Artillery Group, the Cavalry group, and finally Grant himself, were added.

(Near right) The memorial was completed in 1924. It was dedicated in 1922, one hundred years after Grant's 1822 birth.

(Far right) This photograph shows the monument in progress, before its opening.

Theodore Roosevelt Island National Memorial

Washington, D.C.

President, conservationist, Rough Rider: Theodore Roosevelt is a larger than life character in the annals of American history. His 17-foot statue presides over Theodore Roosevelt Island, an island in the Potomac River.

In the 1930s, the Theodore Roosevelt Memorial Association purchased the island, then known as Mason's Island. In honor of the nature-loving president, landscape architects worked to add trails and create a forest environment. The statue and its surrounding pillars and fountains, however, were not added until the 1960s.

The memorial is shown here in 1965 while under construction. Fountains are found in front of the statue.

Franklin Delano Roosevelt Memorial
Washington, D.C.

America's longest-serving president has a memorial that sprawls over 7.5 acres, or 326,700 square feet. It consists of four open-air rooms, each depicting one of his four terms in office. Waterfalls and pools unify the memorial and evoke different events from the tumultuous times that Roosevelt oversaw during his presidency. More than twenty quotations are found around the site.

Landscape architect Lawrence Halprin was chosen to design the monument in 1974; however, because of funding delays, the monument was not dedicated until 1997. President Clinton performed the honors.

FDR is shown with his dog Fala. FDR's pose, and whether he should be depicted in a wheelchair, was a matter of controversy.

A statue of Dust Bowl farmers

A breadline during the Great Depression

Sculptor George Segal contributed this statue of a citizen listening to one of FDR's Fireside Chats.

Water features at the monument

THE STRUCTURE OF WORLD PEACE CANNOT BE THE WORK OF ONE MAN, OR ONE PARTY, OR ONE NATION... IT MUST BE A PEACE WHICH RESTS ON THE COOPERATIVE EFFORT OF THE WHOLE WORLD.

ELEANOR ROOSEVELT
FIRST UNITED STATES DELEGA
TO THE UNITED NATIONS

Eleanor Roosevelt was one of the most influential First Ladies.

The 1997 dedication

Mount Rushmore National Memorial
Black Hills regions, South Dakota

Although the monument was completed on October 31, 1941, it wasn't officially dedicated until 1991, by President George H.W. Bush.

The granite of Mount Rushmore erodes at a rate of about one inch every 10,000 years. This means that the carvings could remain basically intact for millions of years!

Ninety percent of the carving work completed at Mount Rushmore was done with dynamite. About 450,000 tons of rock was removed from the mountain. Borglum is shown here in 1932.

Gutzon Borglum and Supt. inspecting work on face of Washington - Mt Rushmore #40

The Black Hills of South Dakota became famous during the gold rush of the late 1800s, when miners uncovered millions in gold and silver from the mountain range. But by 1923, after the gold became scarce, the popularity of the area waned. So South Dakota state historian Doane Robinson came up with an idea to stir up tourism: he thought that sculpting the likenesses of famous people into the rock of Mount Rushmore would attract tourists.

Robinson gained the support of sculptor Gutzon Borglum, who suggested the sculptures be of four presidents: George Washington, Thomas Jefferson, Theodore Roosevelt, and Abraham Lincoln. These, he felt, would best represent the first 130 years of American history. In 1925, Congress authorized the project, and between 1927 and 1941, Borglum and his team sculpted the four 60-foot-high carvings into the rock.

Today, Mount Rushmore National Memorial is South Dakota's most popular tourist attraction, proving that Robinson's monumental idea worked exactly as he'd hoped.

Borglum's original plan called for the figures to be carved from head to waist, and he wanted to include a map of the Louisiana Purchase. But insufficient funding required him to scale back the carving. This 1936 photograph shows a model of the project.

Around the Country various locations

Presidents are a popular subject for statues that are found throughout the country. The images on these pages represent just a fraction of presidential statues.

Before the Washington Monument began construction in D.C., other monuments existed to memorialize the nation's first president. Two Maryland monuments were much speedier. The one shown on the left, found in Baltimore, Maryland, was begun in 1815 and completed in 1829. The one shown on the right was built in a single day in 1827, by residents of Boonsboro, Maryland.

Franklin Pierce is a more obscure president, but New Hampshire's State Capitol honors its native son.

Tennessee people might be take a special interest in this Raleigh, North Carolina, monument! Presidents Polk, Jackson, and Johnson were all born in North Carolina, though their later careers took them to Tennessee.

A statue of Jimmy Carter is found on the grounds of the Georgia State House. Carter was born in Plains, Georgia.

The "First Lincoln Memorial," built 1909–1911, is found in Abraham Lincoln Birthplace National Historical Park in Hodgenville, Kentucky.

Sam Houston
various locations

Sam Houston held many positions during his lifetime: U.S. Congressman from Tennesee, governor of Tennessee, General in the Texian Army, President of the Republic of Texas, and —after Texas had been annexed by the U.S.— Senator from Texas and governor of that state. The namesake of the city of Houston, he left his stamp on Texas in ways that are still seen today.

The city of Houston remembers Houston with this 1925 equestrian statue found in Hermann Park.

In 1994, this larger-than-life figure was honored with a larger-than-life statue known as *A Tribute to Courage*. Found in Huntsville, Texas, the statue stands 67-feet tall. As they say, "Everything's bigger in Texas."

Buffalo Bill
Cody, Wyoming

At the Buffalo Bill Center of the West, visitors can tour a museum complex to find out about the American West, from its natural history to the stories of the Plains Indians to its art. And, at the Buffalo Bill museum, they can find out about the colorful character who became a legend in his own time. Born William Frederick Cody, "Buffalo Bill" was a Union army scout who became a hunter, trapper, and prospector in the West, and a consummate performer and showman whose Wild West shows mythologized the frontier.

Several statues at the museum complex highlight figures from the West.

Sacagawea

Washakie, a Chief of the Shoshone

Little Turtle, a Chief of the Miami

Buffalo Bill

Harriet Tubman
various locations

"There are two things I've got a right to," Harriet Tubman said, "and these are death or liberty. One or another I mean to have."

Tubman won her liberty—and then turned around and went back into danger repeatedly, risking liberty and life to lead other enslaved persons along the routes of the Underground Railroad. She was an active part of the Union Army during the Civil War, serving as nurse, scout, and spy.

(Right) This 2008 statue by Alison Saar is found in New York City. Images on Tubman's skirt represent the enslaved people she helped escape.

(Above) This Boston, Massachusetts, monument by Fern Cunningham is called *Step on Board.* The back of the monument depicts the route of the Underground Railroad. Inscriptions of quotations said by and about Tubman are also found there, including Frederick Douglass' note, "The midnight sky and the silent stars have been the witnesses of your devotion to freedom and of your heroism."

Frederick Douglass
various locations

Born into slavery, Frederick Douglass "stole this head, these limbs, this body from my master and ran off with them." As orator, author, newspaper publisher, and leading abolitionist, he became a towering figure in the struggle against slavery.

Wanderers through the northwest corner of New York's Central Park will come across a memorial to Frederick Douglass near Central Park North and Frederick Douglass Boulevard. A statue stands in the middle of a large circle with a fountain and granite features. Inscriptions relate incidents from Douglass' life and quotations from his work.

Douglass was the first African American individual to have a monument dedicated to him. In 1899, only a few years after Douglass' 1895 death, the statue was erected in Rochester, New York. Rochester had been Douglass's home for many years, and was the place where he first published his newspaper *The North Star*. The statue is currently found in Rochester's Highland Park.

91

Martin Luther King Jr. Memorial
Washington, D.C.

In 1986, Dr. Martin Luther King Jr.'s birthday was declared a national holiday. Around the same time, the country's first African American fraternity, Alpha Phi Alpha, pushed to have a memorial constructed in Washington, D.C. to honor the late civil rights leader's memory. Ten years later, Congress finally gave the fraternity permission to go ahead with their plans, and they formed a foundation—the Washington, D.C. Martin Luther King Jr. National Memorial Project Foundation—to handle the project.

By 2008, the foundation had raised around $108 million, and construction on the memorial began in 2009. The foundation chose ROMA Design Group in San Francisco to create the design, which was based on a line in King's famous "I Have a Dream" speech: "Out of the mountain of despair, a stone of hope." The centerpiece of the monument is a 30-foot-high sculpture of King, named the *Stone of Hope*. On either side stand two large pieces of granite that symbolize the "mountain of despair." So in a figurative way, visitors pass through the "mountain of despair" to reach the "stone of hope."

OUT OF THE MOUNTAIN OF DESPAIR,
A STONE OF HOPE

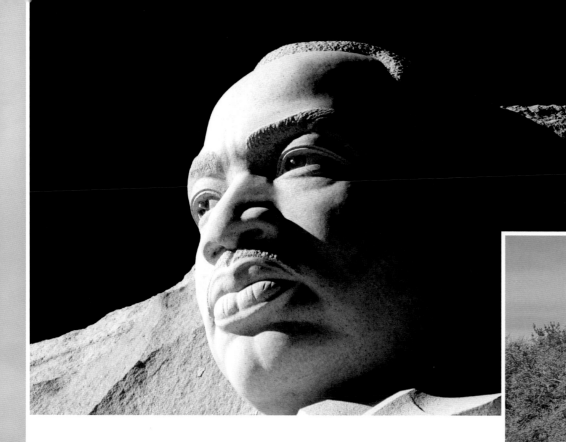

King was the first African American to be honored with a memorial near the National Mall, and one of only four non-presidents—including John Ericsson, John Paul Jones, and George Mason—with memorials in this prestigious location.

The street address of the memorial is 1964 Independence Ave. The "1964" was specifically chosen for the monument in reference to the 1964 Civil Rights Act.

A crescent-shaped inscription wall stands near the memorial, which includes quotes from many of King's speeches. But since the main theme of the memorial is his "I Have a Dream" speech, none of the quotes on the wall are from that speech.

César Chávez
various locations

An activist for laborers and civil rights, César Chávez popularized the slogan "*Sí, se puede*" and co-founded the organization that became the United Farm Workers union. The importance of his legacy is underscored by numerous memorials and honors, from a U.S. postage stamp to the fact that his birthday is a state holiday in multiple states. There are statues of him in places as far apart as Austin, Texas, and Milwaukee, Wisconsin. His presence is felt especially in California, where he lived and worked for many years.

César Chávez Plaza is found in downtown Sacramento, California. The plaza had existed since the mid-1800s, but it was renamed after the activist in 1999, and the sculpture added in 2001.

(Left) Judith Baca's work, *The César E. Chávez Monument: Arch of Dignity, Equality and Justice,* was dedicated in 2008 and is found on the grounds of San Jose State University.

(Below) César Chávez National Monument is found in Keene, California, at the site that served as the headquarters for the United Farm Workers. The Memorial Garden where Chávez is buried is shown here.

(Right) A replica of what served as typical housing for farmworkers can also be seen at the National Monument.

Sports Figures
various locations

Admiration of sports figures unites Americans—when it doesn't divide us! We pin hopes and dreams on our nation's athletes, cheering on our teams and remembering notable players with fondness.

This Babe Ruth statue is found in Baltimore, Maryland, outside of Camden Yards.

This statue of Jackie Robinson, who broke the color line in baseball, with shortstop Pee Wee Reese, is found in Brooklyn, New York.

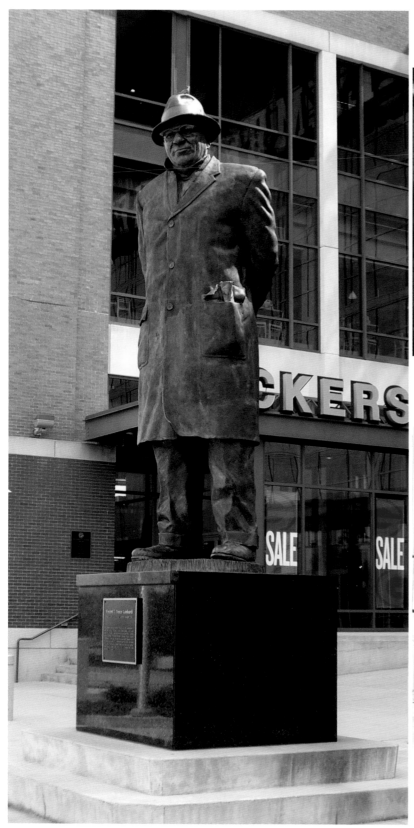

Famous football coach Vince Lombardi is honored with a statue in Green Bay, Wisconsin.

Visitors to the Staples Center in Los Angeles, California, home of the L.A. Kings, can admire hockey action even outside the arena.

Monument to Joe Louis, dedicated in 1986 in Detroit, Michigan, is also known as *The Fist.* It commemorates not only Joe Louis' boxing prowess but also his struggle against Jim Crow.

97

Augustus Saint-Gaudens
1848–1907

Born in Dublin, Ireland, Augustus Saint-Gaudens became a major American sculptor during the second half of the 19th century. He worked on some of the flurry of Civil War memorials that proliferated in the decades following the war, as well as a number of statues of Abraham Lincoln. Later in life, he settled in New Hampshire, where he sponsored a colony of artists. Those grounds are now a National Historic Site, where visitors can view more than 100 of his works.

Augustus Saint-Gaudens in his studio

The Robert Gould Shaw and Massachusetts 54th Regiment Memorial was unveiled in Boston, Massachusetts, in 1897. Robert Gould Shaw was a white Colonel who led the Massachusetts 54th regiment of volunteers: the first unit of African American soldiers. The unit took heavy losses, and Shaw himself died, in the battle at Fort Wagner; the memorial commemorates their bravery, valor, and sacrifice.

The Adams Memorial, also known as *The Mystery of the Hereafter*, is found in Rock Creek Cemetery in Washington, D.C. It serves as a grave marker for Marian "Clover" Hooper Adams.

Not all Saint-Gaudens work was large; he also designed coins, including this $20 "double eagle" gold coin.

Saint-Gaudens did several sculptures of Lincoln; this one is found in Chicago's Grant Park.

One of the sculptor's early commissions, depicting David Farragut, was installed in New York in 1881 (the photograph shows here shows the one at the Saint-Gaudens National Historic Site). Farragut, a naval hero, was the originator of the phrase, "Damn the torpedoes, full speed ahead."

Lorado Taft
1860–1936

Lorado Taft was a prominent sculptor from Illinois who produced a substantial body of public sculpture. Though his works are found throughout the country, there is a strong concentration in the Midwestern states. See page 31 for another of his works.

The Thatcher Memorial Fountain is found in Denver, Colorado, where it has adorned City Park since its 1918 dedication. The name is that of a prominent Denver businessman; the central figure represents the state of Colorado.

Taft worked on the Horticultural Building at the 1893 Chicago World's Fair. Because of the time pressure, some of Taft's female students were given a chance to work on these preparations, which was unusual at the time. Many women of the "next generation" of American sculptors came from this group.

The Fountain of the Great Lakes is situated at Chicago's Art Institute. Five figures represent the five Great Lakes.

Graduates of the University of Illinois at Urbana-Champaign will be familiar with the *Alma Mater* statue.

Patriots (left) and *Pioneers (right)* are paired statues found at the Louisiana State Capitol in Baton Rouge.

Daniel Chester French
1850–1931

Daniel Chester French is most renowned for his work on the sculpture of Lincoln in the Lincoln Memorial *(see pages 78-79)*, but he was a prolific sculptor who left behind an impressively large body of work. A denizen of the East Coast born in New Hampshire and later residing in Massachusetts, Washington D.C., and New York City, he was a contemporary and friend of Ralph Waldo Emerson and the Alcott family.

French's studio, Chesterwood, is a National Historic Landmark found in Stockbridge, Massachusetts.

Installed in 1903 in front of a Columbia University library building in New York City, the *Alma Mater* statue depicts Athena.

Washington D.C.'s Dupont Circle Fountain was installed in 1921. It honors Rear Admiral Samuel Francis Du Pont, who served in the Union Navy during the Civil War.

The Progress of the State is found at Minnesota's State Capitol.

French did a series of sculptures representing four continents for the Alexander Hamilton U.S. Custom House in New York City: *America* and *Europe* are shown here.

Minute Man is found in Concord, Massachusetts.

In 1893, French created *Statue of the Republic* for the Chicago World's Fair (the World's Columbian Exposition).

The 1900s
various locations

Anna Hyatt Huntington (1876–1973) was a groundbreaking artist and a founder of the first public sculpture gardens in the United States, South Carolina's Brookgreen Gardens. She is shown here in her studio in 1965.

When Huntington's *Joan of Arc* was installed in New York City in 1915, it was a rare public monument sculpted by a woman, and also rare for having as its subject a specific historic woman.

Versions of Huntington's *El Cid Campeador* are found in the United States, Argentina, and Spain. This one is found in San Diego.

It runs in the family: Alexander Calder (1898–1976) was the son and grandson of renowned sculptors who created a number of public monuments. *Flamingo* is found in Chicago, Illinois.

Art Deco sculptor Marshall Fredericks (1908–1998) created a number of pieces seen throughout the country, including *Man and the Expanding Universe*, a monument to space exploration located at the headquarters of the State Department in Washington, D.C. See more of his work on pages 118 and 139.

Isamu Noguchi (1904–1988) created not only sculpture but stage sets and furniture. Noguchi's *Intetra*, a mist fountain, is found in West Palm Beach, Florida.

Prison Ship Martyrs' Monument
New York, New York

During the Revolutionary War, the British army imprisoned captured Americans in a set of jails and prison ships in New York Harbor. More than 11,500 Americans died as prisoners of war. The current monument is actually the third at the site; it was dedicated in 1908 by President-elect William Taft. Its single Doric column rises almost 150 feet, topped by a funeral urn lit by an eternal flame. Some of the prisoners' remains are housed in a crypt at the base of the monument.

The current eternal flame at the top of the monument is solar powered.

Architect Stanford White *(shown)* designed the monument, while Adolf Weinman sculpted the funeral urn at the top of the monument and four eagles that stand at its base.

The Titanic Memorial
Washington, D.C.

U nveiled in 1931, Gertrude Vanderbilt Whitney's monument was erected to honor those who died in the *Titanic* disaster—specifically, those men who sacrificed their lives so that women and children could survive. The memorial was sponsored by the Women's *Titanic* Memorial Association, and more than 25,000 American women contributed.

Gertrude Vanderbilt Whitney was responsible for the statue, while Henry Bacon (of the Lincoln Memorial) created the exedra, the circular area surrounding the memorial. Whitney also created the equestrian sculpture of Buffalo Bill found on page 89.

Part of the inscription reads:

TO THE YOUNG AND THE OLD/
THE RICH AND THE POOR/
THE IGNORANT AND THE LEARNED/
ALL/
WHO GAVE THEIR LIVES NOBLY/
TO SAVE WOMEN AND CHILDREN

107

The Irish Memorial
Philadelphia, Pennsylvania

*A*n *Górta Mor*, the Great Famine that took place in Ireland between 1845 and 1852, had a devastating effect on the Irish population. It's estimated that one million people died when potato blight caused the crops to fail, resulting in widespread famine. The disaster also led to a widespread diaspora of another million people. The wave of emigrants who fled the country reshaped the future of not only Ireland but the United States.

The memorial, sculpted by Glenna Goodacre *(see page 47)*, was unveiled in 2003. The 35 figures are arranged in groupings that show starvation in Ireland, the perilous journey, and arrival in the United States.

The Katyń Memorial
Jersey City, New Jersey

In April and May 1940, during the Soviet invasion of Poland, more than 20,000 Polish citizens were slaughtered in the Katyń Forest and left in mass graves. The Soviets later blamed the mass executions on the Nazis, but eventually admitted responsibility in the 1990s. The victims included many soldiers in the Polish Army, including a high percentage of its officers, and also civilians, including hundreds of doctors.

The Katyń Memorial was unveiled in 1991, 50 years after the massacre. Stanislaw "Stanley" Paszul, a Jersey City factory worker—and former member of the Polish Resistance—provided the driving force behind the project. Along with this monument, Polish-American sculptor Andrzej Pitynski later worked on the National Katyń Memorial (2000) in Baltimore, Maryland.

A bronze relief on one side of the statue highlights a related tragedy: Many Polish citizens were sent to Siberia, where they suffered from hunger and harsh conditions. Paszul himself was imprisoned in a Siberian work camp.

Chapter 7: Honoring the Dead
Holocaust Memorials
various locations

Memorials to the victims of the Holocaust are found in all regions of the United States. They show a variety of styles and approaches, as artists grapple with the horror of the murder of millions of people.

George Segal sculpted this memorial found since 1984 at the California Palace of the Legion of Honor. A friend of Segal's who was a Holocaust survivor modeled the figure of the standing man. (San Francisco, California)

Holocaust survivors worked to create and fund the Holocaust Memorial of the Greater Miami Jewish Federation. Designed by Kenneth Traister, it was dedicated in 1990. (Miami Beach, Florida)

The New England Holocaust Memorial, designed by architect Stanley Saitowitz, is shaped around six towers. The number six serves as a reminder of the six million Jews killed, but also evokes the specter of the six main extermination camps. Panels are inscribed with numbers that suggest the numbers tattooed on the arms of prisoners. (Boston, Massachusetts)

Artist Yaacov Agam created a monument comprised of nine panels. As viewers move around the monument, looking at it from different angles, they see different images that explore different aspects of the Holocaust. The monument was dedicated in 2003. (New Orleans, Louisiana)

111

Oklahoma City National Memorial
Oklahoma City, Oklahoma

While not a part of the official memorial, two nearby churches that were damaged in the bombing–First United Methodist Church of Oklahoma City and St. Joseph's Catholic Church–created memorials on their property that are open to the public. St. Joseph's erected the statue *And Jesus Wept.*

On April 19, 1995, the Alfred P. Murrah Federal Building in Oklahoma City was destroyed when domestic terrorist Timothy McVeigh detonated a truck bomb in front of the building. In the days immediately following the attack, a chain-link fence was erected around the rubble, and mourners began leaving flowers, cards, and mementos in honor of the 168 people who lost their lives and the surviving victims.

Just a few months later, Oklahoma City Mayor Ron Norick created a task force to establish a permanent memorial in the Murrah Building's location. And just five years after the attack, the Oklahoma City National Memorial was dedicated.

The focal point of the memorial is the Field of Empty Chairs, which consists of 168 glass, bronze, and stone chairs—one for each victim—with a name etched into each. Also included in the memorial is a reflecting pool and a section of the original chain link fence, where visitors still leave items in remembrance of the bombing.

(Top) The empty chairs are arranged in nine rows to symbolize the nine floors of the building. Each chair is arranged so that it corresponds to where its respective person was located at the time of the bombing.

(Right) A "Survivor Tree" stands on the north side of the memorial. This American Elm was located in a parking lot across the street from the Murrah Building and was nearly destroyed when the bomb went off. But the tenacious tree began to bloom again a year after the attack, and it is now a protected part of the memorial.

The waterfalls that pour into the pools are the largest manmade waterfalls in the United States.

National September 11 Memorial & Museum
New York City, New York

The deadly terrorist attacks on September 11, 2001, killed thousands, shocked the nation, and left the city of New York altered forever. Where the Twin Towers of the World Trade Center once stood, there are now two massive reflecting pools, part of the National September 11 Memorial & Museum. Great waterfalls pour into the pools, with the victims' names inscribed around them.

Public discussion about a memorial began soon after the attacks, with construction following in 2006. The Memorial Plaza opened in September 2011, exactly ten years after the attacks. Family members of the victims were able to view the site on the 11th, with the site opening to the public a day later. The museum, which opened a few years later in 2014, includes physical artifacts from the tragedy, audio and video recordings, and photographs of the victims.

Foundation Hall in the museum contains the Last Column. This beam from the South Tower was removed in 2002, closing out the recovery period. During that recovery period, workers left tributes and photographs on the column, which are preserved at the museum.

Flight 93 National Memorial
Stoystown, Pennsylvania

On September 11, 2001, forty people aboard hijacked United Airlines Flight 93 were determined to wrest control of their plane from the hijackers. Without their intervention, the plane would have caused untold devastation to its intended target, believed to be the U.S. Capitol. The plane crashed sixty miles from Pittsburgh, killing all on board. Congress passed a bill approving the establishment of a memorial in 2002, with the first phase of the memorial dedicated on September 10, 2011. The visitor's center was completed in 2015.

Empty Sky is found across the Hudson River, in Jersey City, New Jersey. The names of 746 victims from New Jersey are inscribed on the monument.

The Memorial Plaza Walkway leads to the Wall of Names. The wall is aligned with the plane's flight path.

The Pentagon Memorial, found outside the Pentagon, consists of 184 benches that represent the loss of the 184 victims of the attack on the Pentagon on 9/11. A group burial marker at Arlington National Cemetery also honors those victims.

Erected in 2006 in Shell Beach, Louisiana, this memorial is paired with a granite plaque listing the 163 residents of St. Bernard Parish who lost their lives during Hurricane Katrina. St. Bernard Parish was one of the areas most affected by the storm.

More than 1,200 people—possibly as many as 1,800—died when Hurricane Katrina swept along the Gulf Coast. It destroyed homes and devastated neighborhoods, as well as having a severe impact on the environment.

Artist Sally Heller created this sculpture, *Scrap House,* which was unveiled in 2009 in New Orleans.

The granite wall of the Hurricane Katrina Memorial in Biloxi, Mississippi, is inscribed with the names of victims. The height of the wall—12 feet—correlates with the height of the water during the peak of the storm surge. A glass case on one side of the monument contains artifacts related to the storm.

Chapter 8: Monumental Faith
Christian Statues
various locations

Statues of Jesus, Mary, saints, and Christian religious leaders appear throughout the United States. Many are found inside or in front of churches; others were personal projects of devotion. Only a small fraction can be included on these pages.

Our Lady of Peace rises more than 30 feet tall, and is located in front of Our Lady of Peace Catholic Shrine in Santa Clara, California.

Desert Christ Park is found in Yucca Valley, California. The project of Antone Martin, it contains sculpted works of Biblical figures and scenes. Martin created the park as a response to the Cold War, urging peacefulness.

A Catholic shrine in Indian River, Michigan, the Cross in the Woods contains a number of statues, as well as a museum that collects nun dolls. The central attraction is the cross itself, sculpted by Marshall Fredericks. Cut from redwood, it is believed to be the largest crucifix in the world.

One of the more challenging monuments to visit in this book, *Christ of the Abyss* is found in Key Largo, Florida—to be precise, submerged off the coastline of that city. A copy of an Italian statue, it was placed in 1965.

Chapter 8: Monumental Faith

This statue is one of a series created by local artist Huberto Maestas: an outdoor Stations of the Cross found in San Luis, Colorado.

This statue of Jesus washing the feet of his disciple is seen by visitors to Witness Park, Pittsburg, Texas.

This reflective labyrinth is found at the Shrine of St. Therese in Juneau, Alaska.

You may not recognize the name Phillips Brooks, but you likely do recognize his work: He wrote the lyrics to the Christmas carol "O Little Town of Bethlehem." This statue is found in Boston's Trinity Church, where the Episcopalian clergyman served for a time as Rector. The sculptor was Augustus Saint-Gaudens *(see pages 98-99)*.

Englishman John Wesley was a founder of Methodism. This statue of him is found in Savannah, Georgia; Wesley ministered to the colony of Georgia for two years in the 1730s.

This Is the Place
Salt Lake City, Utah

In 1847, Mormon leader Brigham Young arrived at what is now called Emigration Canyon. He reportedly said, "This is the right place. Drive on." This Is the Place Heritage Park now stands at that location, accompanied by a monument. The current monument was erected in 1947, and was sculpted by Young's grandson.

The figures of Brigham Young, Heber C. Kimball and Wilford Woodruff are found atop an obelisk. Other groups of pioneers appear below. Young was not only a religious leader but the founder of Salt Lake City, and various locations in the city pay tribute to his memory.

When the illustration *(above right)* was created circa 1899, the Eagle Gate monument was already a fixture. Built in 1859, Eagle Gate marked the entrance to Brigham Young's property. It was remodeled in the 1890s.

Young lived for a time in the Beehive House, so named because of the sculpture of a beehive that tops the building. Bees and beehives are important symbolically in the religion.

Ensign Peak was given its name by Young when he and others climbed it in 1847; the location has religious significance due to its inclusion in Young's visions. The stones used in this 1934 monument were gathered from along the Mormon Trail.

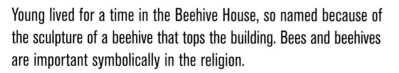

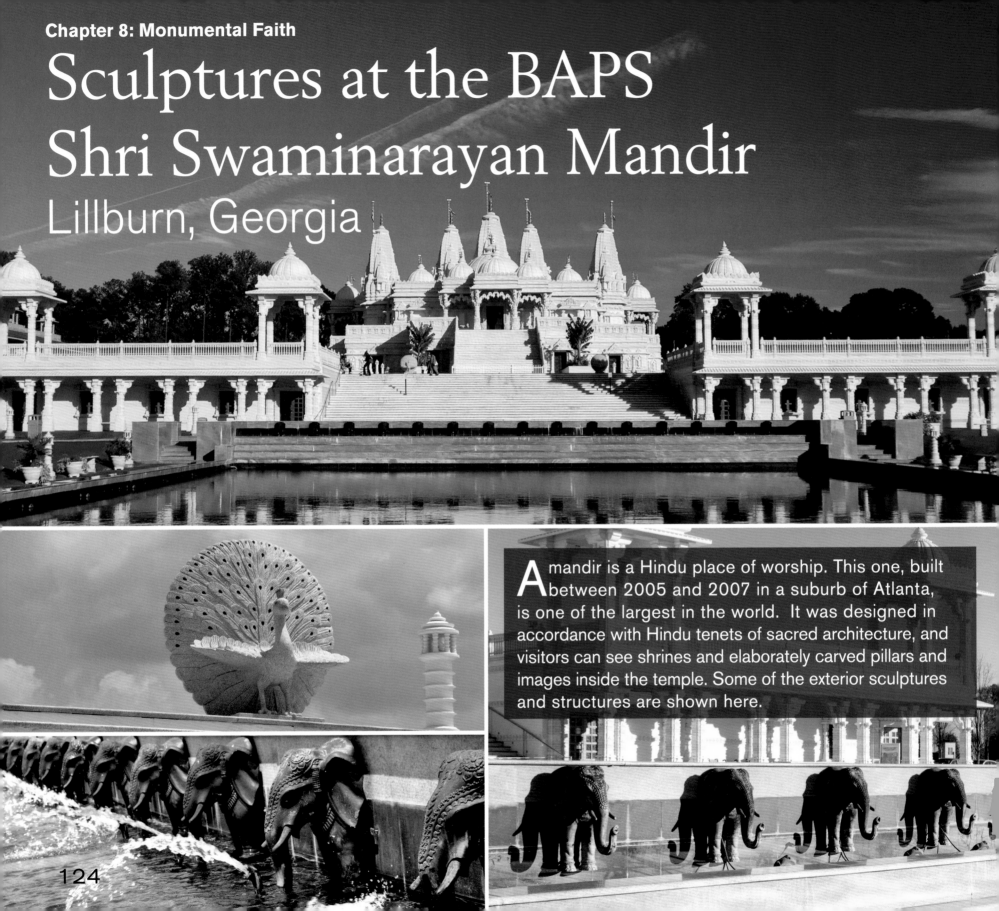

Sculptures at the BAPS Shri Swaminarayan Mandir
Lillburn, Georgia

A mandir is a Hindu place of worship. This one, built between 2005 and 2007 in a suburb of Atlanta, is one of the largest in the world. It was designed in accordance with Hindu tenets of sacred architecture, and visitors can see shrines and elaborately carved pillars and images inside the temple. Some of the exterior sculptures and structures are shown here.

Buddhist Pagodas and Monuments
various locations

(Left) The New England Peace Pagoda is found in Leverett, Massachusetts, and was completed in 1985. It is one of many that were built worldwide after World War II to inspire world peace.

(Right) The five-tiered San Francisco Peace Pagoda was given to the people of the United States by Japan in 1968.

(Left) This statue of the Great Buddha, located in the Chuan Yen Monastery in Carmel, New York, claims the title of largest indoor Buddha statue in the Western Hemisphere.

America's Industries
various locations

Constructed in the 1950s, the Golden Driller stands 75-feet tall in Tulsa, Oklahoma. In 1979, it became that state's official monument. The inscription reads, "The Golden Driller, a symbol of the International Petroleum Exposition. Dedicated to the men of the petroleum industry who by their vision and daring have created from God's abundance a better life for mankind."

Birmingham, Alabama, is home to Vulcan, the world's largest cast iron statue. Standing 56 feet tall and weighing more than 100,000 pounds, it was created for the 1904 St. Louis World's Fair by sculptor Guiseppe Moretti to honor Birmingham's ties to the iron and steel industries. It is shown here at the World's Fair, standing in the Palace of Mines and Metallurgy.

The Beckley Furnace Industrial Monument is found in East Canaan, Connecticut. Now a state park, the site was once home to Beckley Furnace, which operated from 1847–1919 and produced pig iron.

The Silver Valley region of Idaho, also known as the Coeur d'Alene Mining District, was named for its mining heritage. Silver was the primary ore mined, along with zinc and lead. Wallace, Idaho, was one town in that district. The town, where this statue is found, is now on the National Register of Historic Places.

Ames Monument
Albany County, Wyoming

The Ames Monument honors the Ames brothers: Oakes and Oliver Jr., two men instrumental in financing the First Transcontinental Railroad. Oakes Ames was a Congressman who pressed for the monument, while his brother was president of the Union Pacific Railroad. The financing of the railroad later came under investigation, and the monument was to some extent meant to help restore Ames' reputation. The Ames Monument, standing as it does at 8,247 feet, was the highest point on the Railroad at the time. (The Railroad route shifted in later years.) The monument was completed in 1882.

H. H. Richardson designed the monument.

The bas-relief images of the brothers found on the monument were sculpted by Augustus Saint-Gaudens *(pages 98-99)*.

Along the Coastline
various locations

Fishing has long been a risky industry. Monuments have been both celebrated the daring and hard work of sailors and mourned those lost at sea.

Gloucester Harbor in Massachusetts is home to the Gloucester Fisherman's Memorial. The inscription, "They That Go Down to Sea in Ships/1623–1923" is drawn Psalm 107: 23–24, which reads, "They that go down to the sea in ships, that do business in great waters; These see the works of the Lord, and his wonders in the deep."

Currently found on Bailey Island, Maine, this "Maine Lobsterman" statue was created for the 1939 World's Fair in New York.

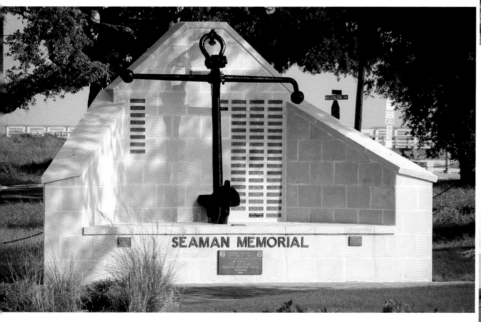

The Seaman Memorial in Ocean Springs, Mississippi, is dedicated to the Mississippi Merchant Mariners.

Barrow, Alaska, the northernmost city in the United States, hosts "The Gateway to the Arctic," a whaling monument.

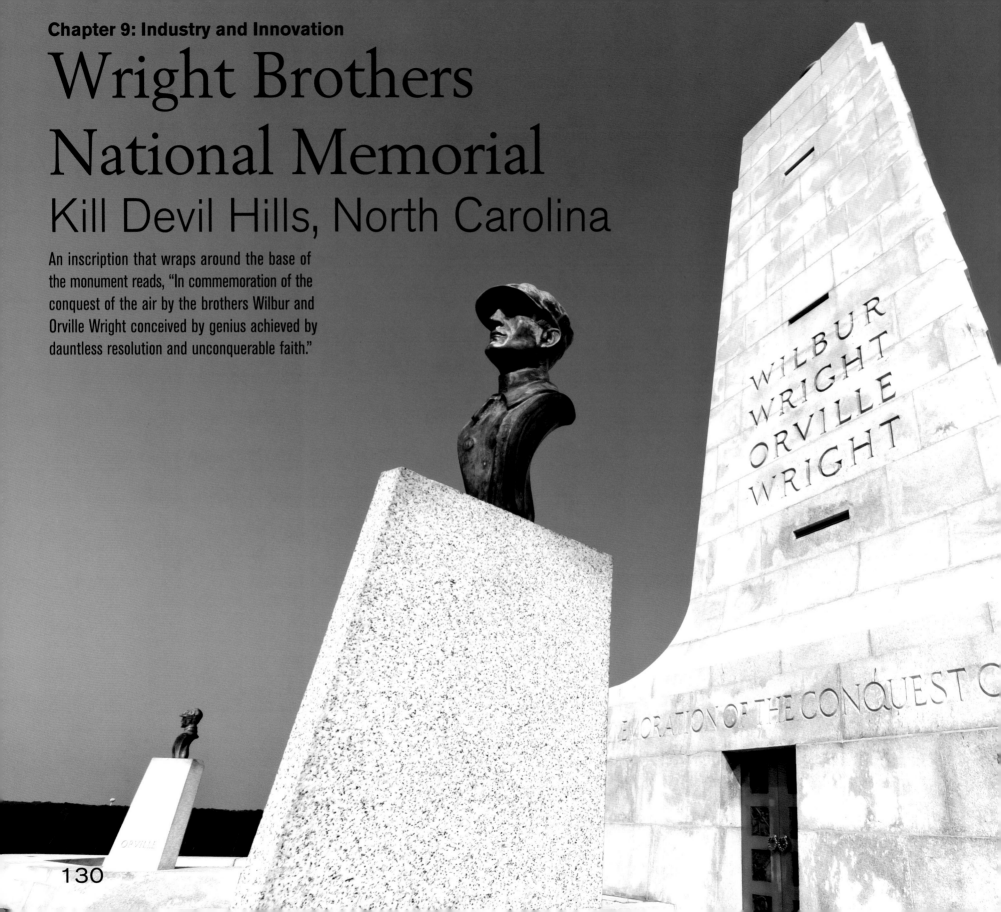

Wright Brothers National Memorial
Kill Devil Hills, North Carolina

An inscription that wraps around the base of the monument reads, "In commemoration of the conquest of the air by the brothers Wilbur and Orville Wright conceived by genius achieved by dauntless resolution and unconquerable faith."

In the 21st century, it's easy to take air travel for granted. But more than a hundred years ago, brothers Wilbur and Orville Wright were just beginning to dream of the possibilities of flight. In 1900, they moved from Dayton, Ohio, to the quiet town of Kill Devil Hills, North Carolina, to fly their experimental planes.

On December 17, 1903, the siblings flew four successful flights, and cemented their place in history. Kill Devil Hills became famous nearly overnight, and earned its motto, "the birthplace of aviation." In the 1920s, President Calvin Coolidge signed a bill that designated $50,000 toward a monument at Kill Devil Hills in the brothers' honor, and construction began in 1931.

In addition to the granite memorial, the site includes markers that designate the starts and finishes of the four flights flown by the brothers.

When the memorial was dedicated on November 14, 1932, Orville Wright attended as a guest of honor. This marked one of the only instances that a national memorial honoree was still alive to attend the unveiling of his own memorial!

The monument stands atop what was originally a 90-foot-tall shifting sand dune where the brothers conducted many gliding experiments. The site was stabilized with special grass and shrubbery, and by the time the 60-foot-tall granite monument was completed in 1932, another $150,000 had been raised to fund the site. Today, the site also includes a visitor center, which features a replica of the brothers' 1903 Flyer.

Winged Figures of the Republic
Hoover Dam, Nevada

Construction on this massive dam began in 1931. During the planning stages, the name Hoover Dam was proposed in honor of the man who was then president. Hoover left office in 1933, however, and the dam continued construction under the name Boulder Dam. Construction continued until 1936: a sweeping, large-scale engineering project that resulted in the death of more than one hundred people.

Franklin Roosevelt, speaking at the dam's dedication in 1935, said, "This morning I came, I saw and I was conquered, as everyone would be who sees for the first time this great feat of mankind.

Ten years ago the place where we are gathered was an unpeopled, forbidding desert. In the bottom of a gloomy canyon, whose precipitous walls rose to a height of more than a thousand feet, flowed a turbulent, dangerous river. The mountains on either side of the canyon were difficult of access with neither road nor trail, and their rocks were protected by neither trees nor grass from the blazing heat of the sun. The site of Boulder City was a cactus-covered waste. The transformation wrought here in these years is a twentieth-century marvel."

In 1947, the dam was officially named in honor of former president Herbert Hoover. Today, Hoover Dam is a National Historic Landmark, which one million people visit each year. Among other wonders, visitors to the site will see the work of Norwegian-born artist Oskar Hansen. Most notably, he developed the *Wings of the Republic*, two winged figures in the Art Deco style placed on either side of a flagpole.

Hansen also produced bas-relief work elsewhere in the dam, including a plaque honoring those workers who died in order "to make the desert bloom."

Construction workers apply a coat of paint circa 1936–1946.

Remembering Local History
various locations

Each state took a different path to statehood, and commemorates events specific to its history. The monuments on these pages look at some of those local histories.

These bas-relief sculptures found on the doors of the Cathedral Basilica of Saint Francis of Assisi trace the history of Santa Fe, New Mexico, and the church itself.

Before Hawaii was a state, it was a kingdom—and Kamehameha I (1782–1819) was the ruler who unified the islands. Several replicas of this statue exist; this version stands in front of Ali'iōlani Hale, now the Supreme Court building but formerly the seat of government.

This statue of John Mullan stands in Mullan, Idaho; it's one of a number of statues and markers found along the Mullan Road in Montana, Idaho, and Washington. Who was the man who gave his name to the place and the road? Lieutenant John Mullan, Jr. (1830–1909) directed the construction of the first wagon road that crossed the Rockies. Built in the 1850s and 60s, the road ran more than 600 miles and was crucial to civilian settlement in the area. This statue is one of a set of thirteen identical statues designed by notable Western artist Edgar Paxson (1852–1919).

Fought in 1836, the Battle of San Jacinto lasted just 18 minutes. Led by General Sam Houston, the Texian Army defeated Santa Anna's army decisively, setting Texas on the path to independence. The San Jacinto monument, built in 1939 at the former battlefield, is topped by the quintessential Texan symbol, the Lone Star. And at 567.31 feet, the obelisk even stands taller than the Washington Monument by about nine feet.

Local Stories of Kentucky

Churchill Downs, the home of the Kentucky Derby, opened in 1875. Its distinctive twin spires were added in 1895, and are shown here in 1901.

In the 1830s and 1840s, Kentuckians suffered greatly from epidemics of typhoid and cholera. Louisville's 1860 Water Tower helped solve that problem. The beauty of its Greek-style architecture helped reconcile doubtful residents to its construction; the link between cholera and typhoid and polluted water was not then fully understood by the public. It holds the distinction of being the oldest ornamental water tower in the U.S.

Currently, the gates are home to a statue of Barbaro, the beloved winner of the 2006 Derby.

The Parthenon
Nashville, Tennessee

In 1897, the state of Tennessee celebrated a century of statehood with the Tennessee Centennial and International Exposition. The city of Nashville, Tennessee's capital, hosted the exhibition. In honor of that city's nickname as "The Athens of the South," a full-scale replica of the Parthenon in Athens was built.

A sculpture of Athena was added in 1990.

Today the Parthenon is found in Centennial Park in Nashville.

This historic image shows the Parthenon during the 1897 exhibition.

Astoria Column
Astoria, Oregon

From afar, this 125-foot column looks simply like an observation tower. At closer range, it tells a story, with murals that wrap along its sides relating significant events from Oregon's history. Dedicated in 1926, it was financed by a railway and Vincent Astor of the influential Astor family; the American Fur company headed by Vincent's ancestor John Jacob had founded Fort Astoria many years prior.

The events detailed in the murals include the expedition down the Columbia River by Robert Gray, the naming of Mount Hood, events from the Lewis and Clark expedition, the establishment of Fort Clatsop, and the arrival of the railway.

Spirit of Detroit
Detroit, Michigan

Dedicated in 1958, the *Spirit of Detroit* is an iconic image representing the city. A Biblical quote from 2 Corinthians 3:17 is inscribed behind the figure of a man: "Now the Lord is that spirit, and where the spirit of the Lord is, there is liberty." In one hand, the figure holds a family; in the other, a sun-like sphere representing the divine.

Sculptor and Michigan resident Marshall Fredericks created both the *Spirit of Detroit* and the *Night and Day* Fountain found in Port Huron, Michigan.

At the State Capitol
various locations

Visit the grounds of your state capitol building—many states host fascinating sculptures and monuments that celebrate the state's history and heroes.

Hartford, Connecticut: Israel Putman, a Revolutionary War hero

Des Moines, Iowa: William Boyd Allison, influential Iowan politician

Cheyenne, Wyoming: Esther Hobart Morris, the first female justice of the peacee

Little Rock, Arkansas: the Little Rock Nine

Trenton, New Jersey: Lady Victory, in the World War II Memorial Rotunda

Columbus, Ohio: The McKinley Memorial, dedicated to Ohio native President William McKinley

Phoenix, Arizona: The Enduring Freedom Memorial honors losses in the Iraq and Afghanistan Wars and the global fight against terrorism.

Famously eloquent statesman and lawyer Daniel Webster presides over the grounds at New Hampshire's State House.

Atop the Dome
various locations

Whille you're wandering the grounds of your state house, don't forget to look up—many buildings have a dome, often topped with an interesting figure.

Ceres, the Greek goddess of agriculture, oversees the State Capitol building in Montpelier, Vermont.

The work of sculptor Daniel Chester French *(pages 78-79 and 102-103)* makes one final appearance on these pages—*Wisconsin* stands tall in Madison, with a badger, the state animal of Wisconsin, perching on her helmet.

Visit Maine's State House in Augusta for a dose of *Wisdom.*

The Sower represents Nebraska's proud agricultural heritage.

Kansas' state motto is *Ad astra per aspera,* meaning, "to the stars through difficulties." Since 2002, the statue *Ad Astra,* depicting a Kansa Native American pointing bow and arrow to the North Star, has adorned the top of the dome.

Independence is a virtue, especially in Rhode Island: *Independent Man* stands atop a dome, paired with an anchor that is Rhode Island's state symbol.

U.S. Capitol
Washington, D.C.

In 1863, the *Statue of Freedom* was added to the top of the dome of the Capitol Bulding. Originally called *Freedom Triumphant in War and Peace*, the statue stands nearly 20 feet tall and weighs around 15,000 pounds. In her hands, she holds a sword, a shield, and the laurel wreath of peace.

The statue had a rocky journey to the top of the Capitol building. The designer, Thomas Crawford, was working in a studio in Rome, but died before he could send the plaster cast model to the United States. When the model was shipped, the trip was delayed by leaks in the ship. The Civil War further delayed its casting. Ironically, one of the casters who worked on the bronze figure was himself enslaved; Philip Reid was later freed in 1862. Finally, the statue was raised in parts to the dome, with the last piece slotting into place on December 2, 1863.

A model of the statue from the 1850s

In 1993, the statue was briefly removed to undergo restoration.